T0329170

Cambridge Elements ≡

Elements in Public Policy

edited by
M. Ramesh
National University of Singapore (NUS)
Michael Howlett
Simon Fraser University
Xun Wu
Hong Kong University of Science and Technology
Judith Clifton
University of Cantabria
Eduardo Araral
National University of Singapore (NUS)

UNDERSTANDING AND ANALYZING PUBLIC POLICY DESIGN

Saba Siddiki
Syracuse University

CAMBRIDGE
UNIVERSITY PRESS

CAMBRIDGE
UNIVERSITY PRESS

University Printing House, Cambridge CB2 8BS, United Kingdom

One Liberty Plaza, 20th Floor, New York, NY 10006, USA

477 Williamstown Road, Port Melbourne, VIC 3207, Australia

314–321, 3rd Floor, Plot 3, Splendor Forum, Jasola District Centre, New Delhi – 110025, India

79 Anson Road, #06–04/06, Singapore 079906

Cambridge University Press is part of the University of Cambridge.

It furthers the University's mission by disseminating knowledge in the pursuit of education, learning, and research at the highest international levels of excellence.

www.cambridge.org
Information on this title: www.cambridge.org/9781108739580
DOI: 10.1017/9781108666985

First published 2020

A catalogue record for this publication is available from the British Library.

ISBN 978-1-108-73958-0 Paperback
ISSN 2398-4058 (online)
ISSN 2514-3565 (print)

Understanding and Analyzing Public Policy Design

Elements in Public Policy

DOI: 10.1017/9781108666985
First published online: June 2020

Saba Siddiki
Syracuse University, New York

Author for correspondence: Saba Siddiki, ssiddiki@syr.edu

Abstract: There has been a surge in scholarship on policy design over the last ten years, as scholars seek to understand and develop existing concepts, theories, and methods engaged in the study of policy design in the context of modern governance. This Element adds to the current discourse on the study of policy design by (i) presenting behavioral assumptions and structural features of policy design; (ii) presenting a multi-level analytical framework for organizing policy design research; (iii) highlighting the role of policy compatibility and policy adaptability in influencing policy efficacy; and (iv) presenting future research recommendations relating to these topics.

Keywords: multi-level analysis, public policy, policy analysis, institutional analysis

ISBNs: 9781108739580 (PB), 9781108666985 (OC)
ISSNs: 2398-4058 (online), 2514-3565 (print)

Contents

1 Introduction

1.1 Policy Design: Definition and Importance for Governance

Public policies are critical for governance. They are the tools that governments use to solve problems that compromise the well-being of citizens (Weimer and Vining, 2011). They signal the priorities of their designers, and ideally the constituencies these designers represent, simply by declaration or through conferring material and nonmaterial rewards and sanctions (Edelman, 1985). Further, policies compel or enable behavior in goal-oriented ways (Schneider and Ingram, 1990). Indeed, policies are intentional. They are deliberately crafted with sensitivity, albeit with varying levels thereof, to features of the problems to which they are applied, assumptions about how individuals inter-pret and respond to behavioral directives, and the broader social, physical, and governance contexts in which they are designed and implemented (E. Ostrom, 2005). And, one would of course be remiss to not acknowledge that policies are ultimately outputs of politics through which it is determined "who gets what, when, and how" (Laswell, 1936).

The purposeful, functional, and normative qualities of public policies all prompt consideration of their design. The study of public policy design is principally concerned with the construction of public policies. For some scho-lars of policy design, the emphasis is on the act of constructing public policies (Linder and Peters, 1989; Howlett et al., 2015). These scholars focus, for example, on decision-making about which instruments to embed within policies to compel behavior toward the attainment of policy goals. Instruments are typically defined as the specific mechanisms through which behavioral response is urged, such as incentives or mandates. These scholars also focus on char-acteristics of the settings in which decisions about instruments are being made, and the implications of such on instrument choice. Other scholars of policy design focus on policies as constructed outputs and are interested in deciphering their attributes (Schneider and Ingram, 1997; Mondou and Montpetit, 2010; Siddiki et al., 2011). From the perspective of these scholars, policy design is defined as the content of policies and how this content is organized (Schneider and Ingram, 1997). To guide their study of policy design, these scholars seek to identify types of content commonly observed across different kinds of policies, qualities of this content, and how policy design links to governance activities, outputs, and outcomes.

To summarize the distinction between the two definitions of policy design, one can employ the following heuristic: policy design as policy formulation focuses primarily on the choice of policy instruments as well as individual, social, political, and other contextual factors that influence instrument choice.

Policy design as content focuses on the structural, functional, and substantive characteristics of this content, in which selected instruments are embedded. Howlett (2014) offers an even simpler distinction: policy design under the two approaches can be conceived of alternatively as a verb or noun. However, while distinct, these two conceptualizations of policy design are also complementary. This complementarity exists, in part, because there are various characteristics of policy design that are applicable regardless of whether one conceives of it as a process or output. For example, irrespective of how policy design is defined, it is recognized that policy design is animated by people. The effectiveness of policy design as a process or output depends in large part on how people interpret and respond to the discretionary parameters articulated within it (Siddiki, 2014). Further, policy designs place into contexts, and contextual incompatibility can lead to conflict that can ultimately undermine effective governance. Context refers to problem, social, economic, physical, historical, organizational, among other, conditions. Context also refers to the broader policy environment. Emphasized in previous, and reinforced in contemporary, policy design studies is that policies are often bundled or mixed with others of similar function and/or intent. When conceiving of policy design as constructed outputs, this observation prompts the need to consider interactions among the structure and content of related polices (Howlett and Rayner, 2007). It can also be useful to consider how different policies that are bundled together to address an issue in a particular domain have evolved over time, and key contextual features that tempered their present-day designs. As Howlett (2014) points out, individual policies that are applied in concert often originate and evolve somewhat independently, and are bundled opportunistically in relation to a particular problem. The implication of this is that policies that are bundled together may be internally inconsistent, or incompatible in their goals, instruments, incentives, or other design features (Siddiki et al., 2018). A related characteristic of policy design that applies across definitions is that it evolves over time as the contexts in which it situates change. These various characteristics suggest the need to consider within the context of policy design studies the issues of policy design compatibility, interactions, policy change, and policy adaptability.

While recognizing that multiple definitions of policy design exist, in this Element policy design is defined as the content of policies. In part, the choice to adopt this definition is reflective of the author's background. The author was trained in theoretical and analytical perspectives oriented in this conceptual definition. This choice is also motivated by developments in scholarship on policy design, in which the distinction between different conceptualizations of policy design has been further clarified, as has the value added of engaging in research that relies on process versus content-based definitions (Howlett, 2019).

A third motivation for defining policy design as content relates to the second. Despite increasing validation and clarification of the value of thinking about policy design as content, theorizing and research on policy design conceived as such is relatively limited. This Element offers guidance on understanding and analyzing policy design as a constructed output. The reasons offered here for treating policy design as content notwithstanding, the Element incorporates insights from scholarship that treats policy design as formulation into the discussion throughout it. This literature can contribute substantially to an understanding of assumptions and features of policy design.

1.2 The Study of Policy Design

The criticality of policy design in the study of governance has inspired a rich body of scholarship on the subject, though this interest has been expressed in bursts over the last several decades. The remainder of this section provides a brief overview of scholarship on policy design, highlighting key shifts in the trajectory of research on this topic. Literature reviews more comprehensive than the one provided in this Element are offered by many other scholars, notably Michael Howlett in his numerous articles, book chapters, and books. Importantly, the literature review that follows provides a description of leading approaches for studying policy design that serves as a basis for the discussion in later sections.

Policy design emerged as a distinct topic of study in the 1960s and 1970s (Howlett, 2017). In scholarship published during this period, policy design was defined both as policy formulation and as policy content. However, the distinction between the two conceptualizations was not always explicitly recognized. As the topic of policy design emerged in prominence, it was broached by scholars with various disciplinary backgrounds, primarily political science, public administration, and economics. The range of policy design–related topics addressed by scholars ostensibly reflected their disciplinary orientations. Scholars of public administration were fundamentally concerned with choices about which instruments to embed in public policies and the role of policy-makers and administrators in these decision processes. Political scientists were chiefly concerned with the politics surrounding policy design. Namely, the types of policies that emerge in different political contexts and the ways in which policies, through their designs, empower or disable groups within society (Lowi, 1964; Linder and Peters, 1989; Skocpol, 1992; Pierson, 1993). Economists were concerned with ascertaining the impacts of instruments embedded in policy design (Kirschen, 1964). There were also prominent theories being applied during this period relating to broader governance issues that borrowed concepts from across disciplines and addressed the topic of policy design. An example is public choice theory, which was leveraged to assess the political and policy dimensions of the production and provision of public services. Scholars of public choice intersected economic, political science, and public administration concepts in seeking to understand, within various domains, which policy designs most efficiently, and appropriately, enabled the effective delivery of public goods and services that markets were unable or unsuited to provide (V. Ostrom, 1962).

The discussion that follows provides a brief overview of some of the leading perspectives on policy design that were introduced in this early period of policy design scholarship, specifically focusing on the work of Lowi (1964) and Wilson (1973). Both Lowi and Wilson contributed to the initial study of policy design by introducing policy typologies, or means for classifying policies generally in terms of what they do and discerning how different types of policies are uniquely shaped by, and shape, the political and/or administrative contexts in which they are applied. As Birkland (2011, p. 209) notes, policy typologies like those developed by Lowi and Wilson "[help] explain policy outcomes by explaining and predicting key aspects of the politics underlying these policies" and further, that, "such typologies are useful in understanding how and why some policies are made the way they are, and why some groups do better than others in policy debates and actual enactment."

Lowi, drawing on the work of Cushman (1941), presented a typology that characterizes the politics associated with three different types of policies: distributive, redistributive, and regulatory. Distributive policies allocate resources to distinct recipients (e.g., individuals, firms) based on closed-door decisions typically involving policy elites. Regulatory policies are intended to prohibit behaviors that pose harm to society, including individual actions that compromise the well-being of others as well as actions undertaken by firms that comprise the competitiveness of economic markets. Policies relating to the former example are referred to as protective regulatory policy, and those relating to the latter, competitive regulatory policy. Regulatory policies elicit support or opposition from interest groups that are variably benefitted or burdened by policies. Redistributive policies transfer wealth accumulated from the general constituency to a smaller group of constituents that share demographic attributes. Redistributive policies are typically designed to promote equity among constituencies, and elicit significant conflict owing to the transference of resources away from one group and toward another.

Wilson's (1973) typology, like Lowi's, captures how policy costs and benefits are distributed across groups within society, but uses this as the primary classifying heuristic. Wilson suggested classifying policies within a two-by-two matrix;

where one dimension captures whether policy benefits are concentrated among very few people or distributed widely among many people, and the other dimension captures whether policy costs are concentrated among very few people or distributed widely among many people. He then associated policy types with interest group politics. He suggested that policies with concentrated costs and benefits will elicit conflict among interest groups that stand to win or lose from a policy; policies with concentrated costs and distributed benefits will generate action by groups who wish to convince policymakers to govern in the public interest; policies with distributed costs and concentrated benefits can indicate close relationships between policymakers and winning interests; and policies with distributed costs and benefits are not likely to provoke focused support or opposition.

The 1980s through the early 2000s saw a theoretical and conceptual concentration in scholarship on policy design around a limited number of theories or orientations, with much of the scholarship falling within one of two tracts. One tract of policy design scholarship focused on identifying and theoretically leveraging generalizable features of policy design. The other tract focused on moving from general classifications of policies, according with Lowi's and Wilson's typological approaches, to characterizing policies in accordance with the instruments embedded within them. Scholars working in both tracts sustained interest in connecting policy design and context (i.e., the social antecedents and consequences of policy design), but it was during this time that the distinction between policy design as formulation and policy design as content was further clarified. In part, this sharpened delineation reflected the distinct foci of policy design scholarship being pursued at that time, which are briefly elaborated as follows.

In 1993, Ann Schneider and Helen Ingram published "Social Construction of Target Populations: Implications for Politics and Policy," in which they presented an analytical framework for evaluating the democratic implications of how policy benefits and burdens are allocated to variably constructed target groups in society through policy designs.[1] Their framework also incorporated a schema for organizing policy design – which they defined in terms of the substance or content of policy – around generalizable elements. These generalizable elements are features of design that are commonly observed across policies applied, for example, at different jurisdictional scales (e.g., local, state, federal) and in different substantive domains (e.g., education, environment, health). In identifying generalizable

---

[1] Anne Schneider and Helen Ingram presented an elaborated description of the framework in 1997 in *Policy Design for Democracy*.

elements, Schneider and Ingram, 1988 enabled systematic comparisons of policy design.

According to Schneider and Ingram (1997), policy designs are commonly constituted of policy goals, targets, tools or instruments, implementation instructions, specific rules of conduct, and an implied causal logic that connects goals, targets, and instruments. Policy goals are the desired outcomes (i.e., broader consequences on social and physical conditions) that a policy is intended to induce. Policy targets are the individuals or groups at whom a policy is directed. Policy tools or instruments are the specific mechanisms that compel behavior. A key premise of Schneider and Ingram's work is that policies, though with varying degrees of coercive pressure, are intended to compel some type of behavior change. This change can be reflected in altered behavior or in the performance of some type of behavior that was previously intended but not actualized. The purpose of policy with respect to the latter is to enable behavior. Given this premise, Schneider and Ingram presented, in connection with their framework, a detailed description of behavioral assumptions relating to different types of policy instruments or tools; that is, expectations about how policy targets are expected to react to different types of policy instruments (Schneider and Ingram, 1990). Implementation instructions direct administrative structure and actions consistent with policy goals. Finally, the embedded causal logic references the soundness of the implied linkage between goals and instruments: in other words, the validity of the reasoning that links the performance of some behavior compelled through the policy instrument by a particular target to the desired policy goal.

In addition to offering a way to characterize common features of policy designs, Schneider and Ingram's framework also offered a policy typology that, like those presented earlier, classified whole policies in terms of general objectives and how policies are intended to compel behavior. According to Schneider and Ingram, policies can be characterized as representing different types of "tools," which they describe as follows (Schneider and Ingram, 1997, pp. 93–95): (i) authority tools, which rely exclusively on deference to authority, without the explicit or even implicit threat of other sanctions; (ii) inducements and sanctions, which encourage "quasi-voluntary" or "quasi-coerced" actions based on tangible payoffs; (iii) capacity-building tools, which provide training, technical assistance, education, and information needed to take policy-relevant actions; (iv) hortatory tools, which consist mainly of proclamations, speeches, or public relations campaigns through which government exhorts people to take the actions needed by the policy; and (v) learning tools, which encourage targets to solve problems. Schneider and Ingram's policy typology is an expanded form offered by Richard Elmore (1987), who distinguishes between the following types of policies, in instrumental terms (an approach which we will discuss in more detail): mandates, inducements, capacity-building, and system-changing. Distinctive about Schneider and Ingram's typology, relative to Lowi's and Wilson's, is that the authors focus less on politics associated with different types of policies and more on behavioral assumptions relating to each (Schneider and Ingram, 1990).

At the same time that Schneider and Ingram introduced and were working to empirically test the validity of their theory of policy design, Elinor Ostrom and others associated with the Bloomington School of Political Economy were pursuing complementary advancements in the study of governing rules as part of their work applying the institutional analysis and development (IAD) framework.[2] The IAD framework, like Schneider and Ingram's social construction framework, offered several approaches for systematically characterizing the rules used to govern behavior according to generalizable features (Ostrom, 2005). Many of the early studies using the IAD framework to study governing rules were focused on tacit or informal rules reflected in social norms and habits. Only in the last ten years has scholarship that uses the IAD framework to study the design of formal rules – such as public policies – flourished (Basurto et al., 2010; Siddiki et al., 2011; 2012; Siddiki, 2014; Carter et al., 2016). Nevertheless, the approaches for analyzing governing rules affiliated with the IAD framework are conceptually and operationally appropriate for studying the design of both formal and informal rules.

The IAD-affiliated approaches characterize the substance of formal and informal rules with varying degrees of granularity. Under one classification approach, rules (which can be constituted of a single directive or a grouping of directives) are characterized as one of three types: (i) operational; (ii) collective choice; or (iii) constitutional. Operational rules identify what specific activities rule targets are required, permitted, or forbidden to perform under certain temporal, spatial, and procedural conditions. Collective choice rules establish processes for making and changing operational rules. Constitutional rules define who is eligible to engage in the design of collective choice rules. Another approach affiliated with the framework classifies individual directives

---

[2] The IAD framework uses the term "institutions" to refer to governing rules. The framework distinguishes between institutions-in-form and institutions-in-use. In the paragraph in which this footnote is placed, institutions-in-form are referenced as formal institutions and institutions-in-use as informal institutions. Another way the framework distinguishes institutions is in terms of strategies, norms, and rules. Strategies, norms, and rules are all types of institutional statements (i. e., statements that assign, with varying degrees of prescriptive force, activities to actors). Strategies are the least prescriptive, assigning activities to actors within conditional parameters. Norms indicate whether these activities are permitted, required, or forbidden. Rules, in addition to assigning prescriptive force to activities connected to different actors, also specify sanctions for noncompliance. This level of institutional distinction was considered necessary in the context of the general discussion of the IAD framework presented in this section of the Element.

according to their functional properties. Under this schema, directives (termed "rules" in the framework) are characterized as (i) position; (ii) boundary; (iii) choice; (iv) aggregation; (v) information; (vi) payoff; or (vii) scope. Position rules identify the absolute number of individuals that can occupy a given position in a decision situation; boundary rules identify the prerequisites or eligibility criteria for occupying positions; aggregation rules relate to joint actions or decisions; information rules indicate channels of communication; payoff rules assign external rewards or sanctions for distinct actions; choice rules articulate specific actions (i.e., what an actor must, must not, or may do) in different decision situations; and scope rules identify required, desired, or prohibited outcomes (Carter et al., 2016). Finally, a third approach for dissecting the content of formal and informal rules, referred to as the institutional grammar, first divides rules (e.g., a public policy) into individual directives and then further parses the content of these directives according to (i) targets; (ii) actions assigned to targets; (iii) the prescriptive operator indicating whether actions are required, permissible, or forbidden; (iv) receivers of action; (v) spatial, temporal, and procedural conditions under which actions are applicable; and (vi) payoffs associated with compliance/noncompliance.

Schneider and Ingram's and Elinor Ostrom's work offered two notable contributions toward the study of policy design. First, it enabled a more precise depiction of the functional and substantive qualities of public policies. Many of the policy design studies published in the 1960s and 1970s characterized whole policies in relation to the broader contexts in which they were developed and applied. This second wave of policy design research offered a platform for thinking about the link between context and *particular* features of policy design. The work of Elinor Ostrom, in particular, highlighted the empirical observation that governing rules are comprised of numerous statements that have varying functional and substantive qualities, but that configure to influence behavior within certain conditions. A second notable contribution of this scholarship was that it opened the door for comparative assessments of policy designs. Having a generalizable set of policy design features meant that analysts had theoretically and empirically informed bases upon which to compare policy designs (Hood, 2007). This ability is particularly important when it comes to studies of policy outputs, outcomes, and effectiveness more broadly.

Turning to the second dominant tract of policy design scholarship developing during the 1980s through the early 2000s, provided here is a brief overview of policy design approaches that reclassified policies in relation to salient design elements. More specifically, this research oriented the study of policy design around instruments, or tools. In this scholarship, policies and the primary instruments embedded within them were used coterminously, and the study of policy design was oriented particularly around understanding the types of instruments governments use in governance, as well as why governments select one type of instrument over another to govern in a particular domain. The descriptive pursuit was enabled by the introduction of new typologies that both reflected and accommodated the growth in types of instruments employed by governments in the 1970s coinciding with increasing privatization and decentralization efforts (Mosher, 1980; Howlett, 2017). Hood (1986), for example, started with a basic delineation among instruments, classifying tools based on their reliance on nodality (i.e., information), authority, treasure (i.e., inducements), or organizational resources. Doern and Phidd (1983) place instruments on a spectrum, ranging from self-regulation to public ownership.

Salamon (1989) and Linder and Peters (1989) were particularly influential in advancing this tract of policy design scholarship. Salamon offered an approach for organizing an expanding array of instruments (e.g., various forms of grants, loans, subsidies, contracting arrangements, etc.) along the dimensions of directness, visibility, coerciveness, and automaticity, though it was not specifically in connection to the study of policy design (Salamon, 1989). Even more generally, Hood (2007) suggests that Salamon was also subsuming organizations and the variable configurations they take in various governance domains under the instrument label. This contrasts with other approaches that only consider policies in their assessment of instruments. Nonetheless, Salamon offered a valuable intellectual basis for understanding the political dynamics associated with instrument choice. Salamon's (2002) *Tools of Government* offered a useful expansion on his previous work.

Linder and Peters (1989) more explicitly connected the characterization of policy in terms of instruments with the study of policy design. They were explicit in their characterization of policy design as policy formulation, and the study of policy design as essentially the assessment of instrument choice. Linder and Peters, like others before them, offered a way to analyze how policy design is influenced by contextual factors. Distinctive about their work, however, was attention to the role of cognition – alongside various features of policy context – in shaping instrument choice. Effectively, Linder and Peters argued that the relationship between context and policy design is mediated by cognitive biases of those engaged in policy design regarding, for example, perceptions of instrument coerciveness and political risk. They presented their approach as enabling multilevel analyses of policy design; specifically, analyses that jointly account for macro- and micro-level factors. As Linder and Peters explain, "micro" pertains to individual decisions and associated calculus about instrument choice, whereas "macro" refers to broader features of the policy process. The following statement conveys their multilevel perspective on viewing policy design studies:

> Characteristics of the political system, such as national policy style, the
> organizational setting of the decisionmaker, and the problem situation are
> all likely to have some influence over the choice of instruments. The relative
> impact of these variables, however, is likely to be mediated by subjective
> factors linked to cognition. Perceptions of the proper "tool to do the job"
> intervenes between context and choice in a complex way. Efforts to account
> for variation in instrument choice, then, must focus not only on macro level
> variables but on micro ones as well. Linders and Peters (1989, p. 35)

Contemporary research on policy design has branched from the scholarship
reviewed hitherto in various ways. In scholarship that defines policy design as
policy substance or content, there has been an enduring interest in applying and
developing the social construction and institutional analysis frameworks introduced, respectively, by Schneider and Ingram and Elinor Ostrom. Those working with Schneider and Ingram's framework have applied it in a variety of cases
to empirically verify the relationship between target group construction and
policy design; namely, that differently constructed target groups experience
variable allocations of policy benefits and burdens through policy design.
However, while there has been substantial effort in clarifying contextual factors
that stimulate changes in social construction and policy design, there have been
few attempts to understand either the antecedents or the consequences of
features of policy design on policy-relevant outputs or outcomes. There has
been a much more robust effort on this front by scholars applying Ostrom's
institutional analysis and development framework to study public policy. Teams
of scholars working with specific analytical methods affiliated with the framework have provided operational guidance for systematically and reliably identifying features of policy design (Basurto et al., 2010; Siddiki et al., 2011); have
linked the presence of certain features, and combinations of features, of policy
design to important governance concepts (Hanlon et al., Forthcoming); and
investigated factors that influence how individuals interpret and respond to
different features of policy design (Siddiki, 2014). One of these analytical
methods that will be addressed in detail later in this Element is the Grammar
of Institutions (Crawford and Ostrom, 1995), also referred to as the Institutional
Grammar Tool (Siddiki et al., 2011) and the Institutional Grammar.

Michael Howlett has inspired the study of policy design from various perspectives in recent years. Howlett acknowledges the multiple definitions of
policy design, though most of his work focuses on policy design as formulation.
Nonetheless, he addresses a variety of practically and theoretically important
concepts that one can explore using either of the policy design definitions
offered earlier in this section. Among them is the concept of policy mixes
(Howlett et al., 2015). Building on instrumentally oriented characterizations

of policy design, Howlett highlights the need to consider implications of the conjoint application of multiple policies, and the instruments embedded in them, within a common domain. One example of this is how these instruments interact to either enable or compromise the attainment of shared policy objectives. In connection with policy mixes, Howlett also raises the importance of considering the developmental trajectories of policies applied in concert within particular domains. Namely, that instruments have distinct origins and contexts that are reflected in their initial and subsequent designs that should be considered as part of an assessment of their interactions. Howlett's most recent research emphasizes the behavioral underpinnings of policy design (Howlett, 2018). In this work, he presents an approach for understanding how policy targets will respond to different types of instruments, given their decision-making tendencies that are not fully captured in utility maximization models.

Within contemporary policy design scholarship, there have also been renewed attempts to classify policies in relation to their dominant policy instruments, and scholars in recent years have continued to offer general ways of characterizing policies in terms of functional qualities. An example is Birkland's (2011) contrast of material and symbolic policies. Material policies confer material rewards and sanctions, whereas symbolic policies convey values and interests of the government without this conference. Such classifications, like those that preceded them, remain useful in identifying the types of qualities along which policies differ.

1.3 Objectives and Contributions of Understanding and Analyzing Public Policy Design

This Element pools insights from scholarship on policy design, with the following specific objectives.

A first objective of this Element is to synthesize insights from scholarship across disciplines, such as public affairs, law, and economics, to highlight the behavioral assumptions and structural features of policy design. The behavioral logic highlights tendencies of decision-making, which have implications for how individuals interpret and respond to the content. of public policies. Structure relates to the "architecture" of policy design, which in this Element is organized into micro, meso, and macro levels. At these different levels, the policy analyst focuses on different features of public policies that convey nonexclusive but distinctive information, and that are generally common to public policies across domain and jurisdictional scales. The rationale for articulating behavioral assumptions and structural features of policy design within this Element is theoretically and practically based. In both policy studies and practice, there is growing interest in how human cognition and psychology influence how individuals interpret and respond to policy (Camerer et al., 2003; Madrian, 2014; Chetty, 2015; DeCaro, 2018). An underlying premise of much of this research is that improved understanding of cognitive and psychological tendencies of individuals operating within rule-governed contexts will help policymakers design better policies; that is, policies that are more likely to be effective at compelling behavior in ways that aligns with policy objectives. But while, in general, behaviorally oriented policy scholarship is ultimately interested in the connection between policy design and behavior, this connection is relatively understudied in policy design scholarship specifically.

The behavioral underpinnings of policy design was minimally, albeit thoughtfully, covered in early policy design scholarship. Among those who explicitly addressed the topic were Schneider and Ingram (1990) who, as discussed in detail in later sections of this Element, posited behavioral assumptions linked to different policy instruments, or tools, that embed in policy designs. In a somewhat contrasting vein, Linder and Peters (1989) addressed the behavioral tendencies of policymakers in their instrument choice. Only recently, in step with broader trends, has the topic of behavioral assumptions reappeared in policy design scholarship (Howlett, 2018). This Element piggybacks on recent trends to refocus policy design in relation to behavioral assumptions, with the intent of synthesizing findings from research that implicitly or explicitly explores the connection from various disciplines. For example, the discussion of behavioral assumptions in this Element incorporates insights from social psychology, and integrates this with scholarship on policy design, to identify and proffer the implications of nondesign-related features in shaping policy relevant decision-making. It draws, for instance, on social psychologist Daniel DeCaro's humanistic rational choice theory, which addresses cognitive factors influencing decision-making regarding cooperation and compliance within rule-governed systems. DeCaro's theory highlights factors such as internalization, acceptance, and perceived appropriateness of rules in fostering cooperation and compliance. His humanistic rational choice theory also addresses the role and importance of socially oriented factors, such as self–other merging.

The rationale for articulating structural features and related approaches for analyzing policy design is more scientifically than practically based. The multi-level analytical framework posited in this Element is meant to provide a basis for orienting new policy design research and existing approaches for studying policy design in terms of their analytical focus. These approaches evaluate public policies at different levels; that is, treat different parts of policy as the focal unit of analysis. While many scholars offer general conceptual similarities among leading approaches for policy design (Howlett and Mukherjee, 2014), to date there has not been an attempt to systematically organize policy design approaches according to the scope of policy that serves as the analytical basis of the approach (i.e., unit of analysis).

A second objective of this Element is to present design-related factors that influence policy efficacy, where efficacy is defined as the achievement of intended results. While existing scholarship points to a host of domain-specific and generalizable factors that influence policy efficacy, this Element focuses on two: policy compatibility and policy adaptability. The motivation for focusing on these two factors in particular is driven by growing recognition in policy studies and related fields of the need to account for the complexity that characterizes real-world policymaking and policymaking environments. Among the various factors contributing to this complexity are the inherent dynamism of social systems, and the contexts in which they are embedded; shared responsibility for policymaking across levels of government; and the observed reality that policy issues are typically addressed through suites of policies, rather than with a single public policy. Adding to this complexity in modern governance is the uncertainty associated with some of our most pressing contemporary governance issues, such as climate change, the incorporation of novel technologies in policy decision-making and public service delivery, and international security. With all of these issues, the scale of their near- and long-term impacts, how they will respond to policy interventions, as well as how individuals will respond to their magnitude, are not fully known. The kind of complexity noted here naturally prompts questions about whether policies developed at different, or the same, levels of government are reinforcing or conflicting in their design, and the implications of such for policy efficacy. Relatedly, it also provokes questions about whether policies applied in concert in a single policy domain are reinforcing or conflicting, and related consequences. Furthermore, complexity owing to dynamism in policy environments raises questions about whether policies are designed to accommodate changing environments and uncertainty, and again, the related implications. The discussion in this Element builds on recent scholarship on policy compatibility and adaptability by identifying ways to operationalize both within the context of policy design.

A third objective of this Element is to present future directions for policy design research. The Element will present future directions for policy design research relating to key themes presented in relation to each of the afore-stated objectives.

Notably, a key contribution of this Element is that it merges theoretical insights from multiple fields in discussing key behavioral and structural dimensions of policy design. The Element will not espouse a particular theoretical or methodological orientation, but rather present a set of theoretically and empirically supported assumptions underlying policy design that are compatible with leading theories and approaches.

1.4 Overview of Sections

Section 2 will cover behavioral assumptions and structural features of policy design, emphasizing the idea that policy design can be analyzed at different levels, with analyses oriented at different levels offering distinct analytical opportunities and constraints. Section 3 will present design-related factors that influence policy efficacy, focusing specifically on policy compatibility and policy adaptability. Section 4 offers an illustrative analysis of two policies leveraging macro-, meso-, and micro-level approaches. Section 5 will summarize key points presented throughout the text, and include suggestions for future policy design research relating to these key points.

2 Behavioral Assumptions and Structural Features of Policy Design

This section addresses behavioral and structural aspects of policy design, and then presents a foundation for understanding how these aspects relate. The behavioral discussion will draw insights from different disciplines to articulate a model of the individual that helps one understand how decision-making tendencies temper the way individuals interpret and respond to policy design. Articulated within this discussion are assumptions about three dimensions of decision-making, which Schlager and Cox (2018) argue are critical for understanding how individuals will ultimately behave in institutionally (e.g., policy) governed situations: (1) what individuals value; (2) individuals' information-processing capabilities; and (3) internal mechanisms that individuals engage when deciding how to act in a particular governed situation.

According to Schlager and Cox, assumptions about what people value essentially reflect how individuals derive utility; i.e., based on private costs and benefits and/or through a consideration of others. Relevant to this dimension are assumptions about how individuals interpret and respond to material and nonmaterial influence and incentives. Information-processing capabilities reflect the cognitive capacity of individuals to process information relevant to a particular decision. However, assuming that individuals are boundedly rational (Simon, 1957), attention to this dimension is less about acknowledging that individuals have limited information-processing prowess, and more about highlighting the types of decision-making heuristics that are engaged in light of it. The discussion in this section relating to this dimension highlights the role of cognitive biases, beliefs, and values in shaping policy interpretation and response. Finally, assumptions about internal mechanisms reflect how decision-making tendencies interact with features of decision contexts to shape behaviorally relevant outcomes. These assumptions reflect, for example, perceptions of the fit of governing rules, the attainment and effect of fundamental needs (e.g., perceptions of procedural justice, competence, belonging), and intrinsic motivations. The discussion of behavioral assumptions will mostly focus on policy targets, but some discussion will also be dedicated to describing assumptions relating to policy designers.

The structural discussion will describe different levels from which to assess policy design – i.e., macro, meso, micro – and the analytical value gained from pursuing assessments at these different levels. The section will conclude by suggesting implications of the articulated behavioral assumptions for studying policy design at different levels.

2.1 Behavioral Assumptions of Policy Design

The questions of how and what individuals value are of enduring interest to policy scholars (Jones, 2001; Jenkins-Smith et al., 2018) and are typically answered within policy scholarship with reference to one of two dominant models of decision-making: the rational actor model, a derivative of rational choice theory; and the boundedly rational actor model (Simon, 1957). Two key assumptions underlie the rational actor model. The first assumption is that individuals are utility-maximizing agents, making decisions that will yield the highest material return given a limited contribution of inputs. A second assumption of the rational actor model is that individuals make utility-maximizing decisions in the context of complete information. In other words, individuals enter into decision situations knowing all there is to know on what they are making a decision, as well as the consequences of their decisions. For this reason, a related assumption of rational decision-making is that preferences are static over time. One would only expect preferences to change if a decision-maker had the possibility of encountering new information (e.g., experience, data, feedback, etc.).

In contrast, the bounded rationality model expands the scope of what is valued by decision-makers beyond private costs and benefits expressed in material terms, to also include non-material costs and benefits (e.g., shame, reputation, interpersonal reciprocity). Additionally, the bounded rationality model of decision-making also addresses information processing faculties of individuals. First, assumed under this model is that individuals do not have access to complete information regarding their decisions. A second, related, assumption is that individuals are cognitively constrained in their ability to process the limited amount of information they have exposure to. Individual preferences are thus expected to be unstable, shifting as individuals are exposed to new information. Even within these various constraints, however, the bounded rationality model assumes that individuals seek to make the decision that will maximize their more broadly construed utility given the informational, cognitive, and other constraints they face at the time of decision-making. This process, yielding an adequate, though perhaps not optimal, outcome is termed satisficing.

A third assumption associated with the bounded rationality model of decision-making, and related specifically to the assumption that individuals have limited information-processing capabilities, is that individuals rely on various types of cognitive heuristics, or filters, to help them process information. One type of cognitive filter is attitudes, which can be reflected in beliefs or values, (Jenkins-Smith et al., 2018) with the consequential tendency that individuals accept information that is consistent with their preexisting attitudes, and effectively sort out information that counters them. This tendency, known as biased assimilation, has been studied extensively in the context of political argumentation [see, for example, Munro and Ditto (1997)].

Additional factors presumed to influence individual decision-making are offered by DeCaro (2018), who presents another alternative to the rational choice theory and its embedded model of decision-making, called the humanistic rational choice theory. DeCaro's theory outlines various cognitive factors influencing decision-making regarding cooperation and compliance within governed systems to help answer questions such as, when and why do individuals under-comply with mandates, or conversely, when and why do individuals over-comply with voluntary standards? This theory views decision-making in rule-governed contexts (where rules can be formal or informal) as rooted in perceptions of fundamental needs, such as procedural justice, self-determination, competence, belonging, and security. It also views decision-making as influenced by intrinsic motivations, such as acceptance (i.e., perceived appropriateness of rule-directed behaviors within the context of broader norms) and internalization (i.e., perceived accordance of rule-directed behaviors with one's beliefs). The concept of acceptance has also been addressed by others; for example, by March and Olsen (1995), who refer to it in terms of a logic of appropriateness, and by Young (2002), who refers to it as institutional fit. The concept of internalization has also been addressed by others such as Ryan and Deci (2000). Finally, existing scholarship also highlights relational or group cognitions that influence how individuals respond to governing rules. Among these are perceptions of interpersonal trust, shared understanding, and self–other merging (Beratan, 2007; DeCaro, 2018). DeCaro defines self–other merging in terms of perceived belonging to group. The concept of group cognitions can even be extended further to encapsulate, generally, the role of culture, context, and history in shaping human cognition and the influence of such on responses to governing rules (Hutchins, 1995).

The preceding discussion links to policy design in various ways. DeCaro's humanistic rational choice theory is explicitly tied to decision-making and related behaviors in rule-governed environments, but a more explicit explanation of how other models and theories of individual decision-making link to policy design is warranted. An overarching point to consider is that assumptions regarding individual decision-making are important given the intentionality of policy design. As Schneider and Ingram note within their own discussion of behavioral assumptions linked to different policy tools, "Public policy almost always attempts to get people to do things they otherwise would not have done, or it enables them to do things they might not have done otherwise" (Schneider and Ingram, 1990, p. 510). Taking this premise as true, policy design should reflect choices about the most effective means to compel behavior in different situations, given how individuals are expected to make decisions and behave.

Schneider and Ingram (1990) offer specific behavioral assumptions linked to authority tools (i.e., instruments), incentive tools, capacity tools, and hortatory tools (see Section 1 for Schneider and Ingram's definitions of these types of tools). According to Schneider and Ingram, authority tools leverage individuals' responsiveness to leader–follower relationships and organizational structure they deem as legitimate. Loyalty and duty are also relevant in the context of authority tools. Inducements rely on individuals' sensitivity to tangible payoffs. Capacity tools address informational constraints that challenge policy decision-making or action by providing means for information provision. Capacity tools can also be used to convey skills and resources to enable policy-related action. Hortatory tools appeal to decision-making heuristics that individuals employ in the face of information-processing constraints and internal mechanisms. Schneider and Ingram effectively convey this sentiment:

> [H]ortatory tools assume that people are motivated from within and decide whether to take policy-related actions on the basis of their beliefs and values. Individuals bring into decision situations cultural notions of right, wrong, justice, individualism, equality, obligations, and so forth. Many of the values, then, that individuals perceive in the decision situation are beyond the control of incentive-based policy tools. Symbolic and hortatory tools assume that target populations are more apt to comply with behavior desirable from policy perspective if the targets see that behavior as consistent with their policy beliefs. Schneider and Ingram (1990, p. 519)

Recent research by Howlett (2018) offers an alternative discussion of behavioral assumptions – what he refers to as demand-side considerations of policy design – linked to different types of policy tools. He does so by connecting relevant behavioral considerations to four types of policy tools identified by Hood (1986): nodality, authority, treasure, and organizational tools (see Section 1 for Hood's definitions of different of tools). Howlett posits that nodality tools rely on perceptions of accuracy of information being conveyed, or "credibility." Howlett posits that authority tools rely on perceived "legitimacy" of government. Treasure, or inducement, tools elicit perceptions of financial need and receptivity to government need; what he refers to generally as "cupidity." Finally, Howlett suggests that organizational resource tools draw on individuals' perceptions regarding whether government can faithfully enable administrative entities and actions to execute policy actions.

Howletts's recent attention to behavioral assumptions linked to different policy tools reflects a growing interest in behavioral science in recent years among economists as well as policy scholars (Camerer et al., 2003; Thaler amd Sunstein, 2008; Madrian, 2014; Chetty, 2015). This line of research, in relation to policy design specifically, explores how psychological and cognitive factors influence policy-relevant decision-making and behavior. Pragmatically, scholarship in this area highlights the design and use of alternative policy instruments that better account for underlying psychological and cognitive assumptions of decision-making, along with, or instead of, traditional instruments. Most prominently highlighted is the role of nudges, which are intended to alter the choice architecture that individuals face in decision situations to less forcefully, but sometimes more effectively, compel behavior toward desired policy ends. Nudge-based policy instruments, unlike mandates or inducements, for example, neither require nor forbid behavior and do not rely on material incentives to compel behavior (Loewenstein and Chater, 2017). Instead they rely, for example, on framing, adjusting the scope of choice sets, and communicating personalized as well as more easily accessible information to decision-makers (Madrian, 2014). Indeed, behaviorally rooted policy approaches are often designed to respond to informational constraints facing decision-makers. A couple of points worth noting here are that even though nudges are the most popularized behavioral policy intervention, Loewenstein and Chater (2017) emphasize that nudges are just one policy approach that draws on insights from behavioral economics, and that the two should not be used synonymously. Further, they argue that though the features of decision-making that behavioral approaches reflect tend to generalize across time and place, it is still important to consider the tempering effect of social, structural, and other contextual factors as well.

As discussed in Section 1, the link between cognition, behavior, context, and policy design was posited in early policy design scholarship, most prominently by Linder and Peters (1989). However, unlike the scholarship referenced in the preceding discussion that focuses on behavioral assumptions that influence how individuals process and respond to policy information, Linder and Peters focus on behavioral assumptions that influence those involved in crafting policy designs. As they note, "interest is concentrated on how [policy] instruments are viewed by actors inside and outside of government who make choices about them and, more specifically, in the criteria used by those actors to judge the suitability of instruments for addressing policy problems" (Linder and Peters, 1989, p. 36). A fundamental interest of theirs is to posit the relative influence of context versus general instrument preferences in shaping the decision-maker's domain specific policy choices. Linder and Peters contend that attributes of the political, policy, and organizational environments in which policymakers operate, as well as attributes of the problems for which they are designing policies, are likely to impact their instrument preferences. However, they argue that alongside these contextual features, even as moderators of the effects of such, are various factors linked to cognition; for example, perceptions of particular instruments that generalize across contexts, ideological orientations, and subjective valuation and evaluative criteria of policy instruments.

Also addressing behavior in connection with policy design from a different perspective than the scholarship reviewed in the early part of this section, but useful for consideration, is work by Sabatier and Mazmanian (1980) on policy implementation. Sabatier and Mazmanian present an implementation framework that identifies problem, statutory, and nonstatutory-related factors that influence policy implementation. Among their problem-oriented factors are two that relate to policy target behavior; specifically, the diversity of behaviors being targeted by a particular policy and the extent of behavior change prompted by policy. They posit that implementation will be challenged with relatively higher degrees of both behavioral phenomena. In their framework, statutory factors accord with policy design. They summarize these factors vis-à-vis behavior and implementation outcomes in the following way:

> [L]egislation that seeks to significantly change target-group behavior in order to achieve its objectives is most likely to succeed if (1) its objectives are precise and clearly ranked; (2) it incorporates a valid causal theory; (3) it provides adequate funds to the implementing agencies; (4) the number of veto points in the implementation process is minimized and sanctions/inducements are provided to overcome resistance; (5) the decision-rules of the implementing agencies are biased toward the achievement of statutory objectives; implementation is assigned to agencies that support the legislation's

objectives and will give the program high priority; and (7) the provisions for outsider participation are similarly biased through liberalized rules of standing and by centralizing oversight in the hands of statutory supporters. Sabatier and Mazmanian (1980, p.548)

Carter et al. (2016) specifically operationalized the framework in relation to policy design.

Finally, recent research that addresses policy mechanisms within the context of policy design studies also offers useful insights about how individuals behave in response to public policy. This research is fundamentally concerned with the process of designing policies and, in particular, the analytical strategies that designers use in this process (Busetti and Dente, 2016). Hence, the relevance of this research within the discussion of behavior in this section of the Element. Indeed, this research builds on research that examines policy implementation from a top-down perspective, such as the work of Sabatier and Mazmanian previously referenced. It clarifies, within this tradition, the motivations that inform the actions of those engaged in policy implementation. Busetti and Dente (2016) highlight that those engaged in policy implementation networks – including politicians, bureaucrats, and social and private actors – all have their own agendas, which may or may not be consistent, and will strive for autonomy. These tendencies will influence their implementation decisions. In drawing attention to such factors, Busetti and Dente are essentially directing attention to the causal mechanisms that underlie how policy designers and others engaged in policy implementation behave. In the spirit of Sabatier and Mazmanian, Busetti and Dente emphasize the importance of understanding causal mechanisms relevant in the context of policy design to ultimately improve the likelihood that policy targets behave in ways intended to enable to attainment of policy goals.

2.2 Structural Features of Policy Design

This subpart will discuss levels at which public policy designs can be analyzed. Relatedly, it will also (i) identify structural features of policy design that can be used as the basis of analyses situated at different levels; and (ii) organize leading approaches for studying policy design by level of analysis.

2.2.1 Analyzing Structural Features of Policy Design at Different Levels of Analysis

In describing key features of the analytical framework in more detail in this part, Gibson et al.'s (2000, p. 219) descriptions of scale and levels of analysis are instructive:

Scale refer[s] to the spatial, temporal, quantitative, or analytical dimensions used by scientists to measure and study objects and processes. Levels on the other hand refer to location along a scale. Most frequently, a level refers to a region along a measurement dimension. Micro, meso, and macro levels refer broadly to regions on spatial scales referring to small, medium, and large-sized phenomenon.

In the multilevel analytical framework detailed in this Element, scale is the scope of policy that one analyzes to pursue research objectives, ranging from the individual policy directives – such as "Actor A must perform X activities under Z conditions" – to whole policies, or the full aggregation of individual directives comprising public policies. Under the framework, levels then refer to different scopal values, of which three are explicitly identified (micro, meso, macro). Policy design assessments, and/or approaches, that treat individual policy directives as the focal unit of analysis, while treating these directives as constitutive of generalizable subelements, are characterized as micro-level. Those that treat individual directives as a whole, or configurations of policy directives, as the focal unit of analysis, are characterized as meso-level. Those that treat whole policies as the focal unit of analysis are characterized as macro-level.

The kind of scale and related levels included in the multilevel analytical framework represents an inclusive nested conceptual hierarchy. Gibson et al. (2000, p. 220) define inclusive hierarchies as the following: "Inclusive hierarchies involve orderings whereby phenomena grouped together at any one level are contained in the category used to describe higher levels, but having no particular organization at each level." Inclusive hierarchies are different than constitutive hierarchies, which Gibson et al. (p. 220–221) describe in the following way: "In [constitutive hierarchies] the lower level can combine into new units that have new organizations, functions, and emergent properties. In complex, constitutive hierarchies, characteristics of larger units are not simple combinations of attributes of smaller units, but can show new collective behavior [or] new and unexpected phenomena." The multilevel framework presented in this Element is inclusive in the sense that policy directives discerned at the micro-level aggregate in the formation of configurations of directives assessed at the meso-level, which further aggregate to form whole policies.

Importantly, the benefits of the multilevel analytical framework extend beyond descriptive classification. Indeed, the classification supported by the framework inherently conveys that analyses situated at different levels offer distinctive analytical leverage for the study of policy design. Relatedly, different types of research questions associate with different levels of analysis.

The following sections describe approaches for studying policy design that situate at macro, meso, and micro levels based on their analytical foci. They also describe the distinctive analytical leverage associated with macro-, meso-, and micro-level policy design assessments.

2.2.2 Macro-Level

Macro-level assessments of policy design treat whole policies as the unit of analysis. Existing policy design scholarship offers multiple approaches that situate at the macro-level. Common among these approaches is that they classify whole policies as being of a particular type based on design features (e.g., dominant instruments embedded within them), function (e.g., allocation of resources), or relationship to context (e.g., political antecedents or consequences). Importantly, classification of policies along these, and other, dimensions prompts consideration of how policies relate to each other (Steinberger, 1980). The classification schemes observed in this body of scholarship, which characterize policies in such macro-level terms, are referred to as policy typologies. They are relevant for the study of policy design for two main reasons. First, typification of policy logically prompts some attention to qualities of policy design. Second, scholarship on policy typologies in many ways provided the basis for policy design research.

The literature review on policy design provided in Section 1 of this Element references leading policy typologies. These typologies are again reviewed here. In this section, however, instead of redefining the typologies, the discussion focuses on the bases for classifying policies within these typologies. The rationale for this focus is that dimensions of policy that serve as a basis for classification of whole policies as being of one type or another are proximately linked to policy design. Further, the broad utility of policy typologies is rooted in how applicable differentiating bases are across policies observed in different domains. The typologies featured in this section were selected because they are generalizable; meaning they are not linked to any particular policy domain (e.g., energy, metropolitan governance).

Table 1 offers a list of leading policy typologies and summarizes how policies are classified under each. Anderson's (1977) policy typology distinguishes between substantive and procedural policy. Substantive policies are those that articulate policy goals within a particular domain and an approach for achieving these goals, for example, through the establishment of a program or establishment of mandates or incentives for compelling certain behaviors. Procedural policies pertain to the work of government; specifically, by detailing the processes by which government personnel are expected to conduct their work.

Table 1 Leading Policy Typologies

Author	Classification within Typology	Dimension of Policy Serving as Basis of Classification
Anderson (1977)	Substantive, procedural	Function
Edelman (1985)	Material, symbolic	Allocation of resources
Lowi (1964)	Regulatory, distributive, redistributive	Function, allocation of resources, political antecedents, and consequences
Kiser and Ostrom (1983)	Constitutional, collective choice, operational	Function
Schneider and Ingram (1997)	Authority, inducements/ incentive, capacity-building, hortatory, learning	Function
Wilson (1979)	Concentrated benefits–concentrated costs, diffuse benefits–concentrated costs, concentrated benefits–diffuse costs, diffuse benefits–diffuse costs	Allocation of resources

Policies are thus specifically differentiated by functional properties. Edelman (1985) distinguishes between material and symbolic policy. As the names suggest, material policies confer tangible sanctions or rewards to relevant policy targets, whereas symbolic policies serve as means for conveying public values, priorities, or emotive appeals. The primary basis for differentiating among policies is thus the allocation of resources. Lowi (1964) differentiates between regulatory, distributive, and redistributive policies. Generally, he defines regulatory policies as those that are intended to curtail harm by establishing order and prohibiting behavior, redistributive policies as those that reallocate resources among groups in society on the bases of group characteristics, and distributive policies as those that allocate resources among groups within society with the intention of benefitting a relatively small group of beneficiaries. Lowi also differentiates policies based on the types of politics they generally elicit and other political characteristics affiliated with them (e.g., the nature of stakeholder dynamics, visibility of policy process). As such, the basis for Lowi's classification is multidimensional; it accounts for policy function, allocation of resources, and political antecedents and consequences. Ostrom (2005) distinguishes governing rules (including policies, but also those not codified in writing) as constitutional, collective choice, or operational. Operational rules most proximately govern the behavior of rule targets, specifying what they are required, forbidden, or allowed to do in particular situations relevant to a particular domain. Collective choice rules delineate protocols for developing operational rules. Constitutional rules dictate who is allowed to participate in collective rulemaking activity. Thus, the main criteria for deciphering rules according to the Ostrom approach is function.

Schneider and Ingram (1997) offer a typology that distinguishes between authority, inducement/incentive, capacity-building, hortatory, and learning policies. Authority policies compel action by way of perceived standing, inducement-based policies encourage behavior through the articulation of tangible payoffs, capacity-building policies provide resources to enable policy-relevant actions, hortatory policies exhort behavior rather than compel it by mandate or conferrence of material rewards or sanctions, and learning policies encourage problem-solving by policy targets. The basis for differentiating policy is based on function. Finally, Wilson's (1974) typology distinguishes between four types of policies: those with concentrated benefits and concentrated costs, diffuse benefits and concentrated costs, concentrated benefits and diffuse costs, and diffuse benefits and diffuse costs. His typology accounts for how widely or narrowly policy costs and benefits are distributed, and thus allocation of resources is obviously the principle dimension upon which policies are classified.

Of the three dimensions that the typologies covered in Table 1 rely on as bases for categorizing policy, two – function and allocation of resources – are arguably directly tied to policy design. That is, these are indiscernible without . evaluation of the content of policy. Not clearly specified in connection with any of these typologies are clear instructions on how to approach, organize, or interpret the content of policies to identify relevant dimensions for the purpose of classification. Nevertheless, policy typologies fit into a discussion of the structural features of policy design because they are based on generalizable properties of policy design. Across any domain, one can generally view the relevance of characterizing policies in relation to each other based on functional properties, or if and how they allocate resources among applicable policy targets. Insofar as content is recognized as part of the structural qualities of policy design, policy typologies can be viewed as providing macro-level lenses of policy design structure.

It is also worth noting that the policy typologies presented in this section have been criticized for various reasons beyond that already recognized. While the typologies continue to be referenced for their more abstract conceptual value, they have not been used extensively to guide empirical inquiry as previously noted. Some of the critiques levied against the reviewed typologies generalize across them, challenging the perceived validity of typologies broadly. The most pronounced among them is the criticism that policies tend not to fall squarely into the different categories included within typologies because multiple types of policies can have shared characteristics (Linder and Peters, 1989; Smith, 2002). In other words, policies, by their definitions, are not conceptually distinct. Illustrative of this point is the difficulty in distinguishing between distributive and redistributive policies using Lowi's typology. Both types of policies are fundamentally intended to allocate public resources among different sets of constituents. Smith (2002) suggests that one way to overcome the noted criticism is to further engage in the use of taxonomies in place of typologies. Smith differentiates the two as follows: whereas typologies, like those included in Table 1, rely on differentiation among policies based on conceptual grounds, taxonomies encourage differentiation based on empirically observed policy characteristics. While the taxonomical approach may help address the aforementioned validity concern, it introduces concerns of generalizability.

2.2.3 Meso-Level

Meso-level policy design analyses focus on individual directives as a whole, or configurations of policy directives, that convey policy-relevant meaning. They assume, drawing on observed reality, public policies have common elements that are reflected in the content of individual or groupings of directives. By way of contrast, whereas macro-level approaches for assessing policy design take whole, distinct policies and characterize them as being a particular type based on some defining characteristic, meso-level approaches aim to identify elements of policy design that generalize across policies from various domains. Another way to conceive of the difference between macro- and meso-level approaches, is that macro-level approaches such as the policy typologies covered previously are engaged in inter-policy classification; meso-level approaches elicit intra-policy classification. In so doing, meso-level approaches prompt attention to particular directives embedded within policies – statements, clauses, provisions, etc. that indicate what specific actors must, may, or must not do under certain conditions – or combinations of these directives that together convey particular types of information or meaning.

Schneider and Ingram (1997) and Ostrom (2005) both offer approaches for engaging in meso-level assessments of policy design, that complement their macro-level approaches reviewed in Section 1 and in the preceding subsection.

Table 2 Meso-Level Policy Design Classification Approaches

Author	Classification within Typology	Dimension of Policy Serving as Basis of Classification
Schneider and Ingram (1997)	Goals to be solved Target populations Implementation agents and infrastructure Policy tools (instruments) Operational rules	Function
Ostrom (2005)	Position rules: Identify roles to be filled by individuals Boundary rules: Identify prerequisites for occupying positions Choice rules: Specify specific actions Aggregation rules: Address collective decision-making and activity Information rules: Govern communication and information flows Payoffs: Assign rewards or sanctions for specific actions Scope: Identify required, desired, or prohibited outcomes	Function

Their meso-level classification schemes are described in Section 1 and are briefly summarized in Table 2. Continuing with the theme from the discussion of meso-level approaches, Table 2 also indicates that the basis for distinguishing directives, or suites of directives conveying a particular type of information, is functional property.

   Schneider and Ingram's meso-level policy classification approach, while not necessarily offering clear instructions on deciphering policy elements, requires policy analysts to engage in some level of organization of content, beyond what would be the required application of macro-oriented policy typologies. If not a thorough investigation of each of the various directives that constitute policy designs, their approach at least urges the analyst to consider types of element-related information conveyed by groupings of these directives. Ostrom's approach prompts more detailed consideration of individual directives, essentially necessitating formal identification of individual directives comprising public policies, and subsequent assessment of functional properties of each and accordant classification.

Important to note are fundamental differences in the utility one gleans from macro-level approaches for evaluating the structure of policy design prompting inter-policy classifications and meso-level approaches focused on intra-policy characterizations. Macro-level approaches can be useful for yielding information about how different policies within shared or different domains relate on some qualitative basis. Meso-level approaches, which are geared primarily toward intra-policy classifications, allow the analyst to evaluate how different elements or directives embedded within policy designs relate to each other. Beyond offering descriptive value, this ability enables evaluative assessments of policy designs along various normative dimensions. For example, it allows analysts to determine the coherence or internal consistency of policy designs (Sabatier and Mazmanian, 1980). As noted by Schneider and Ingram, a distinct benefit of their approach is the ability to glean insight on the implicit causal logic reflected in policy designs regarding the relationship between goals, targets, and instruments (i.e., the logic that presumes that compelling certain targets' behavior through chosen instruments will result in the attainment of stated policy goals). Ostrom's meso-level approach is fundamentally rooted in the notion that in order to understand how a governing rule is intended to guide the behavior of targets within decision situations, the analyst must consider how directives constituting governing rules (e.g., policies) with different functional properties link together to inform such.[3] According to Ostrom's framework, any decision situation is governed by some combination of position, boundary, choice, aggregation, information, payoff, and scope rules. Accordingly, the role of the analyst following a classification of policy directives would be to identify focal decision situations and the array of the different types of rules that structure it.

In closing this subsection, meso-level approaches to evaluating policy design, by moving down in levels of abstraction in the identification of policy design features – offer distinct benefits relative to macro-level approaches; in part by helping address some of the operationalizability and empirical applicability concerns raised in relation to macro-level approaches. First, their generalizability derives from two sources: both the utility of using function as a

---

[3] These decision situations are referred to as "action situations" by Ostrom under the overarching framework she developed for the study of governing rules, which the meso-level approach described in this subsection is affiliated with. The name of this framework is the institutional analysis and development framework.

basis for classification as well as the commonality of design elements across policies. Second, even while using function as a classifying heuristic, meso-level approaches offer clearer conceptual distinctions between policy design elements being classified. The elements/rule types specified under Schneider and Ingram's and Ostrom's approaches, respectively, largely convey distinctive information. This is associated with higher validity, and potentially, empirical reliability. Importantly, both approaches have been leveraged in empirical studies of policy design. Ostrom's approach has also been used extensively in the study of governing rules reflected in social norms, cultural practices, or what could be classified as informal governing rules. Third, the more precise accounting of policy design features accommodates a systematic comparison of policies, in ways that macro-level approaches do not.

2.2.4 Micro-Level

Micro-level policy design analyses focus on individual policy directives as the unit of analysis, but, unlike meso-level approaches that evaluate whole directives, micro-level analyses treat directives as constitutive of generalizable subelements that are also assessed as part of the analyses. The following provides further articulation of the contrast between micro-, meso-, and macro-level policy design analyses. Whereas macro approaches focus on classifying whole policies on certain generalizable bases, and meso-level approaches focus on deciphering and characterizing individual policy directives or configurations of directives that provide specific types of information commonly conveyed in public policies, micro-level approaches focus on dissecting and classifying the content of individual policy directives along generalizable categories. This section covers an increasingly popular policy analysis approach developed by Crawford and Ostrom (1995) to parse the linguistic content of the individual directives constituting governing rules in accordance with a generalizable syntax.[4] They refer to this syntax as the "Grammar of Institutions," but the analytical technique has also been referred to as the Institutional Grammar Tool (Siddiki et al., 2011; 2012) and the Institutional Grammar (Siddiki et al., Forthcoming). Crawford and Ostrom developed the institutional grammar in recognition that directives have common structural elements, with each element conveying certain semantic meaning relevant for understanding how directives are intended to shape behavior. According to Crawford and Ostrom, directives

---

[4] In place of "directive," Crawford and Ostrom use the term "institutional statement," which they define as the following: "a shared linguistic constraint or opportunity that prescribes, permits, or advises actions or outcomes for actors (both individual and corporate). Institutional statements indicate, with varying degrees of prescriptive force, specific actions that actors are required, permitted, or forbidden to perform, within certain temporal, spatial, or procedural conditions."

included in governing rules are typically constituted of the following syntactic elements. One of the elements, the Object, was added by Siddiki et al. (2011).

[1] *Attribute-* which conveys to whom the directive applies. The Attribute performs the action, or set of actions, indicated in the statement.

[2] *Aim-* the action(s) that the Attribute is linked to.

[3] *Object-* animate or inanimate receiver of the action in the statement.

[4] *Deontic-* a prescriptive operator (e.g, must, may, must not) that indicates whether the action identified in a directive is required, permitted, or forbidden.

[5] *Condition-* the temporal, spatial, or procedural conditions(s) associated with different actions.

[6] *Or else-* a payoff associated with performing, or failing to perform the action of the statement.

For illustrative purposes, consider the following example directive pertaining to the regulation of organic farming: "Operations certified as organic under the National Organic Program must submit an organic systems plan annually or face certification revocation." This statement would be deconstructed as follows in accordance with institutional grammar syntax: *Attribute* = "operations certified as organic under the US National Organic Program"; *Deontic* = "must"; *Aim* = "submit"; *Object* = "organic systems plan"; *Condition* = "annually"; *Or else* = "or face certification revocation."

Crawford and Ostrom posit that most directives that are intended to regulate behavior (assign Y actions to X actor) will contain at least an Attribute (actor), Aim (action), or Condition (parameters of activity).[5] Those that are more prescriptive in force, will also contain Deontics (prescriptive operator), and an Or else (payoff). Noting the more or less prescriptive qualities of directives has not just descriptive significance for Crawford and Ostrom, they also posit the behavioral significance of having different linguistic structures of directives. A basic assumption linked to varying structural features, is that directives with Deontics and/or Or elses are more coercive, and in the case of the latter alter the expected payoffs of complying with directives, and are thus likely to elicit different behavioral responses from policy targets than directives that lack these elements. In connection with this assumption, Crawford and Ostrom also present guidance on how to model Deontic interpretation by Attributes, accounting

---

[5] Directives found in policy can take a regulatory or constitutive form (Carter and Weible, 2015). Regulatory and constitutive directives take syntactically distinct forms. Regulatory directives assign actions to actors (e.g., "X must do Y under Z conditions"). Constitutive directives are declarative or establish something. They typically take the following forms: "There is X" or "X is Y [under specific Conditions]."

for various internally and externally sourced motivations that affect it. Examples of internally sourced motivations offered by Crawford and Ostrom are feelings of guilt or shame that an Attribute harbors from noncompliance with a directive. Examples of externally sourced motivations include fear of social approval or loss of reputation or standing from noncompliance.

Like meso-level approaches for assessing the structural features of policy design, micro-level approaches like Crawford and Ostrom's accommodate intra-policy classification, and particularly the ability to understand how different directives relate to one another. Once policy analysts have dissected the syntactic structure of policy directives, identifying the content associating with each syntactic element, they can then begin to aggregate and compare information across directives to gain a comprehensive understanding of, for example, the complete set of actors to whom a policy applies (i.e., policy targets), the complete array of activities assigned to policy targets, individually and collectively, and the amount of behavioral discretion afforded to policy targets.

One of the greatest benefits of micro-level approaches to studying policy design, relative to macro and meso-level approaches, is the precision with which they allow analysts to capture key elements of policy design. Greater precision requires clear conceptual distinctions; that is, clarity in how structural elements differ. Crawford and Ostrom's institutional grammar, for example, clearly conveys the semantic differences between information according with different syntactic elements of policy directives. Another benefit of precision is that it is more useful in empirical assessments of how policy design features link to important governance outcomes, for example, in analyzing behavioral outcomes, like policy compliance.

Finally, before concluding this section, it is worth discussing the sole emphasis herein on the institutional grammar. The primary reason for this is that the institutional grammar is presently the only theoretically grounded approach that has been used by a sizeable community of scholars to study the language (i.e., words and phrases) of individual directives constituting the designs of public policy. That is, the number of studies published in recent years that employ the institutional grammar to explicitly study policy design, suggests that it is increasingly recognized as a versatile policy design analysis tool. Scholars have used other approaches to engage in the micro-level assessment of policy design. For example, Mondou and Montpetit (2010) use propositional analysis to analyze the propositional statements comprising Canadian poverty policies to derive theoretically relevant policy design patterns. Just as institutional directives are the focal units of analysis and are comprised of multiple syntactic components conveying distinctive meaning under the institutional grammar, propositional statements are the unit of analysis in propositional analysis and are comprised of four syntactic elements – an issuer, a connecting verb, an object, and a receiver (Mondou and Montpetit, 2010). However, the singular or relatively limited application of this and other approaches for studying policy design specifically suggests analytical appropriateness not analytical trend. Indeed, the application of the institutional grammar to the study of policy design is part of a larger research program, which is being led by scholars who are committed to developing it theoretically and methodologically (Siddiki et al., 2019). The field is thus likely to continue to see an increase in applications of the institutional grammar in coming years, making attention to it in this Element in the context of micro-level analyses helpful.

2.3 Synthesizing Behavioral Assumptions and Structural Features of Policy Design

This subpart will discuss the implications of behavioral assumptions specified in Section 2.1, articulating a model of the individual, in relation to micro-, meso-, and macro-level depictions of policy design.

A key underlying premise motivating this discussion is that individuals respond to policies based on their mental model, though expectations about how they do will be more or less abstract depending on the level of analysis at which one is investigating policy design and associated links to behavior, as well as the conceptual approaches on which they rely for assessing this link. Given this premise, briefly revisited here are the individual decision-making assumptions presented at the beginning of this section. Individuals are assumed to be boundedly rational; they value and account for tangible and intangible rewards and sanctions in their decision-making. In the face of cognitive constraints that limit their information-processing capabilities, individuals employ heuristics in interpreting and sorting externally delivered information and stimuli. In essence, these heuristics act as filters of information that individuals are exposed to. Examples of such include beliefs and values. In addition to these individual assumptions that generalize across decision situations, the preceding discussion also identifies various assumptions about how individuals make decisions in rule- (e.g., policy-) governed contexts specifically. Among them, how individuals respond to directives is influenced by perceptions of the appropriateness of these directives for the domains in which they are being applied, and group cognitions regarding how individuals relate to others.

In macro-level assessments seeking to link policy design and behavior, the analyst can pose only general assumptions about how individuals might respond to policies of a particular type. Cognitive heuristics such as beliefs and values linked to the role of government, the distribution of resources among society, and equity or fairness may be particularly informative. Further, assuming information-processing limitations, it is unrealistic to assume that individuals are either aware of, or fully comprehend, the entirety of directives of which a public policy of a particular type is comprised. In the context of meso-level analyses, where the analysts are looking at groupings of directives that convey specific types of meaning, the cognitive information-processing task is notably less burdensome. As such, while constraints in information processing may limit individuals' ability to interpret multiple sets of configurations of directives, they are likely to understand how information and incentives from a discrete number of related directives pertaining to a particular activity interact to govern their behavior. Finally, in the context of micro-level assessments, it can be reasonably assumed that individuals are capable to interpreting and responding to specific material incentives embedded within directives comprising policies, as well as their degree of coerciveness, indicated by language conveying prescriptive force (e.g., must, should, may). Given the granular focus on specific policy directives, policy targets are confronted with fewer information-processing demands. Material incentives are easier to identify and process, though individuals may have a limited understanding of the consequences of pursuing actions as indicated in policy directives. Within the context of assessments included at any of three analytical levels, one can assume that policy specific factors – e.g., perceptions of policy fit, group cognitions – would be relevant in shaping individual decision-making and action.

3 Policy Design and Policy Efficacy

This section will present design-related factors that influence policy efficacy, focusing specifically on: (i) policy compatibility, and (ii) policy adaptability.

3.1 Policy Design Compatibility

This subsection will discuss the link between policy compatibility and policy efficacy, as well as ways for operationalizing policy compatibility leveraging policy design. The discussion in this subpart will focus broadly on two types of policy compatibility: inter-policy compatibility and intra-policy compatibility. Inter-policy compatibility refers to the extent of alignment on policy design elements (e.g., goals, instruments, incentives, syntactic elements) among policies that govern common and different subjects, targets, and policy issues. Intra-policy compatibility relates to soundness of the causal logic embedded within policy designs that links policy goals, targets, and instruments and the behavioral tendencies of policy targets. The discussion in this section builds on the content presented in Section 2 presenting structural features of policy design.

3.1.1 Linking Policy Compatibility and Policy Efficacy
Inter-Policy Compatibility

Argued in this section is that compatibility among elements observed within and across policy designs is important to consider in assessments of policy efficacy. Inter-policy compatibility is relevant in any domain in which multiple policies are applied in concert to address a common issue or set of issues. Policymakers often simultaneously apply multiple policies in a particular domain to achieve policy objectives (May et al., 2006; Yi and Feiock, 2012; Howlett et al., 2015). Indeed, rarely is an issue deemed worthy of public attention addressed using only a single policy. It is far more common for policymakers to apply suites of related policies that address the same or different dimensions of a given policy issue.

In recognition of this, policy scholars have sought to examine the design and/ or interacting effects of policies comprising policy suites. In policy scholarship, these suites of policies have been referred to as policy bundles (Kassekert and Feiock, 2009), policy mixes (Gunningham and Sinclair, 1999; Howlett and Rayner, 2007), policy toolkits (Howlett et al., 2015), and policy portfolios (Doremus, 2003; Gunningham et al., 1998), among others. Central to scholarship on the idea of policy suites, conceptualized using these various terms, is considering the potentially interacting effects of related policies. More specifically, ascertaining whether the designs of the individual policies within a suite, bundle, or mix are reinforcing or conflicting. May et al. (2006, p. 382) use the term "policy coherence" to refer to how well policies with similar objectives fit or go together.

Howlett et al. (2015) situate a focus on policy suites, defined as policy toolkits, within a "new policy design orientation." According to Howlett et al., the old policy design orientation took a mostly instrumental or tool-based approach to studying single policies, particularly in relation to implementation issues and processes. In contrast, the new policy design orientation focuses on "complex tool preferences … and also devotes more attention to the temporal processes which brought existing policy tool mixes into being" (Howlett et al., 2015, p. 293). In their discussion of the new policy design orientation, they draw attention to the work of Gunningham et al. (1998) and others interested in synergies and conflict among policy mixes, bundles, portfolios, etc.:

> Gunningham et al. (1998) had already led tools-oriented scholars to focus on how instruments within a policy mix or "portfolio" could complement each

other or conversely, lead to conflicts, resulting in guidelines for the formulation of more sophisticated policy designs in which complementarities were
maximized and conflicts avoided ... While this work has continued, concerns
regarding how to make the most of policy synergies while curtailing contra-
dictions in the formulation of new policy packages has become a major topic
of investigation within the new design orientation. Howlett et al., 2015, p. 297

Noting temporality and inter-policy compatibility, Howlett et al. highlight
another focus of the new policy design orientation – to understand the evolution
of individual policies and groupings of policies. A key premise of scholarship
with this focus is that policy evolves incrementally, such that the current designs
of policies retain many of the elements of previous policy iterations. Combining
individual policies into mixes that may generally orient toward a common
general objective does not overcome policy legacies that favor particular tools
and goals. The result is that individual policies within policy mixes may have
contradicting tools and goals. Doremus (2003, p. 217) argues that in the context
of policy mixes, or what she refers to as policy portfolios, it is important to have
goal clarity, systematically monitor and evaluate policy effectiveness, remain
sensitive to the policy context, and revise the portfolio in accordance with new
policy-relevant information.

Intra-Policy Compatibility

Of the many critical elements of policy design highlighted by scholars is the
implied causal logic that undergirds it. This logic reflects assumptions about
how different elements of policy design relate to one another and, more
specifically, about the potential for policy instruments to support the attainment
of policy goals, given assumptions about how policy targets are expected to
behave. More basically, this is the logic undergirding the supposition that policy
targets engaging in the behavior compelled by the instrument articulated in the
relevant policy design will result in the attainment of the policy objectives.
Schneider and Ingram (1990, p. 68) define this causal logic in the following
way:

> The underlying structural logic contained in empirical examples of policy
> refers to the pattern in which the elements of policy occur, or the patterns
> through which policies address problems or seek to achieve goals. Just as it is
> possible to diagram a sentence linking together the parts of speech, it is
> possible to diagram the structural logic of a policy by showing the relation-
> ships among these elements.

Policy efficacy is, in large part, predicated on the soundness of the causal
logic underlying policy design. When this causal logic is lacking in integrity, the

potential for observing disagreement in expected and actual policy behavior, or disagreement in expected and actual policy impacts, is heightened. Lack of intra-policy compatibility can thus be conceptualized as a policy outcome informed by a misspecification of the link among the causes of a problem and the solutions designed to address it. When considering intra-policy compatibility from an inter-temporal perspective – or deterioration of the causal logic informing policy design over time – it can also indicate a failure to incorporate policy feedback or learning.

Finally, a lack of intra-policy compatibility may stem from faulty assumptions regarding the behavior of policy targets, upon which policy design decisions are based. As noted by Siddiki (2018) regarding the link between policy design and policy efficacy, insecure foundations to relating to the behavioral assumptions underlying policy design have related descriptive and normative implications. The descriptive implication is a revealed mismatch between expected and actual behavior. That is, there is disagreement between how policy targets are expected to behave and how they actually do behave, which could be informed by inappropriate behavioral assumptions. The normative implication concerns the consequences of this mismatch. Operationally, behavior that is out of sync with policy directives is considered noncompliance. Noncompliance is salient insofar as it can undermine the attainment of broader public policy objectives. In such cases, actual policy impacts conflict with desired policy impacts.

3.1.2 Operationalizing Compatibility through Policy Design

As noted in Section 2, meso- and micro-level approaches for analyzing policy design are particularly instructive in assessments of intra-policy compatibility. In treating policy design elements and directives as essentially configural in nature – that is, in assuming that they work together to convey policy relevant information – they are well suited for the purpose of ascertaining how internally coherent policies are in their designs. They can at least be useful to analysts in organizing the content of policies to more readily determine the soundness of the causal logic that connects different policy design elements.

Further, while from a typological perspective, meso- and micro-level approaches are positioned in Section 2 as primarily being useful for engaging in intra-policy classification, they can also be usefully leveraged for the purpose of examining inter-policy compatibility. Foremost, these approaches accommodate such examinations because they rely on identification of common features of policy designs, along which they can be compared. For example, using Schneider and Ingram's meso-level typology of policy design elements, the analyst can determine how multiple policies compare in their goals, targets, instruments, implementation instructions, etc. Using Crawford and Ostrom's institutional grammar, the analyst can systematically compare how individual policy directives with some common bases (e.g., targets, issue foci, types of information conveyed) compare in their syntactic structure; for example, in how much behavioral discretion they afford. Behavioral discretion can be operationalized as the relative frequency of different types of prescriptive operators/ Deontics (e.g., must, may, must not) or the relative abundance of temporal, spatial, or procedural parameters/conditions within which policy-related activities can occur. These opportunities remain prospective at the moment, as they have not been empirically availed yet to a great extent. However, Siddiki et al. (2018) illustrate how Schneider and Ingram's typology of policy design elements can be used to analyze compatibility among federal and state vehicle environmental performance standards that have common foci and common targets (i.e., the behavior of specific policy targets is simultaneously governed by the federal and state policies). Siddiki et al. characterize and compare the goals, instruments, and incentives of federal and state policies to examine whether the policy directives, and the design elements that they configure to constitute, compromise the ability of policies from different levels to achieve their stated objectives.

3.2 Policy Adaptability

This subsection will address the relationship between policy adaptability and policy efficacy. A key premise of the discussion in this section is that policies are applied in dynamic settings and those that accommodate dynamism in the information, political, biophysical, and other types of contexts in which they are applied are more likely to sustain their effectiveness. Further, that policies can be designed to be more or less "receptive" to external stimuli.

3.2.1 Linking Policy Adaptability and Policy Efficacy

As noted by Young (2013, p. 9), "Once established, governance systems do not become unchanging or static arrangements. All governance systems … are subject to change over time arising from shifts in the character of the problems to be solved, changes in the nature and capabilities of the actors involved, or developments in the broader setting, including the rise of new discourses and the emergence of new technologies." This note rings louder in our modern governance era, in which some of the most serious issues we face are simultaneously complex and uncertain. Issues ranging from climate change mitigation and planning, to governance of emerging technologies (e.g., autonomous machines and systems), to regulating the use of data collected through social media applications, have one notable commonality: they pose unknown externalities – both positive and negative. Policymaking for such issues evokes a shift in our dominant governance paradigm: from one that is centered on governing for, and indeed, fostering static conditions, to one to that pivots on governing for uncertain conditions.

Public policies are important mechanisms through which policymakers can seek to govern adaptively, in response to uncertain conditions or the kinds of contextual changes noted by Young. As more general points, whether, and with what frequency, policy designs change can signal responsiveness to contextual changes. How they change can signal a wide range of phenomenon relevant in the study of governance broadly, for example, the issues and types of information that policymakers value, who exerts control of the policymaking agenda, and legislative or administrative capacity to enable policy change.

Scholars studying adaptation in relation to policy design conceive of the ways that policies can be designed to facilitate their adaptability in light of new information, altered problem contexts, changing political dynamics, among other factors (DeCaro et al., 2017). DeCaro et al.[6] identify the following types, or features of laws, that enable adaptation: (1) Reflexive laws containing legal sunsets that encourage iterative decision-making. Operationally, reflexive laws are those that establish goals and standards while leaving the paths for achieving them unspecified, as well as those that stipulate planned periods of policy evaluation. Legal sunsets essentially specify term limits for the applicability of policies, or certain policy provisions, at which policymakers can thoroughly evaluate the use and design of delimited policies; (2) Formal delegation of authority for stakeholders with policy domain specific expertise to participate in policy deliberation and decision-making. This type of delegation is viewed as enabling the flow of new information into the policymaking process that may elicit the need for policy adjustment. The motivating presumption here is that knowledgeable stakeholders may be particularly well aware of such kinds of information; (3) Formal delegation of responsibility

---

[6] DeCaro et al.'s discussion of legal design is situated within a broader discussion of adaptive governance, which they describe as a governance approach that recognizes "the needs for systemic change, and incorporates elements of learning (e.g., experimentation), collective cooperation, and human ingenuity" (DeCaro et al., 2017, p. 2). They also define adaptive governance processes as "flexible, e.g., open to revision, iterative decision-making, and experimentation; innovative; participatory; and polycentric, or spread over multiple centers of activity, social networks, and environmental stakeholders in a pluralistic decision-making context" (DeCaro et al., 2017, p. 3). Their discussion of legal design suggests that policies applied in the context of adaptive governance would also exhibit these same features. Further, that these features are what encourage policy adaptability, or changes to the design of a policy that respond to alterations in the contextual conditions.

for stakeholders with policy domain specific expertise to participate in policy deliberation and decision-making. In contrast to formal delegation of authority that grants stakeholders the right to engage in policy activities that could enable adaptation, delegation in responsibility formally vests these stakeholders in these activities; and (4) Tangible support, taking the form of either technical or financial support, to enable delegation of responsibility to stakeholders and/ or governance units that are geographically or operationally close to the issues being addressed through public policies. Importantly, for DeCaro et al., policy efficacy is framed not just in the attainment of specific outputs, outcomes, and impacts tied to the goals of a policy, but also to the extent that they promote other relational objectives, such as self-organization, coordination, and colla-boration across scales (DeCaro et al., 2017). These latter objectives are them-selves viewed as improving policy adaptability.

Similar to DeCaro et al., Swanson et al. (2010) also identify qualities of policy design that enable adaptability, but their conception of policy design refers to both definitions of policy design offered in Section 1; namely, policy design as policy content and policy design as the crafting of policy. Consistent with the general argument posited in this section linking policy adaptability and efficacy, they offer the following arguments:

> Public policies have an important role to play in fostering [the ability for people to adapt to change]. But for policies to be effective and to help people, the policies themselves must also give careful consideration to complex interactions and be able to adapt to conditions that can and cannot be anticipated. A policy that is unable to continue to perform in a dynamic and uncertain setting, or unable to detect when it is no longer relevant, is a policy that is more likely to hinder the freedom and capability of people to adapt to change. Swanson et al., 2010, p. 924

Swanson et al. identify the following features of policy design that enable policy adaptability: (1) integrated and forward-looking analysis; (2) built-in policy adjustment; (3) formal policy review and continuous learning; (4) multi-stake-holder deliberation; (5) enabling self-organization and social networking; (6) decentralization of decision-making; and (7) promoting variation. According to Swanson et al., integrated, forward-looking analysis in the policy designing process involves consideration of multiple policy futures, or scenarios, accord-ing to which built-in policy triggers can be embedded into the actual content of policy. Such built-in policy triggers specify policy adjustments that would be implemented should various conditions envisioned in scenario planning. Formal policy reviews, which can be stipulated within the content of policy, involve assessments of policy performance, as well as create opportunities for discussing whether and how policies are likely to perform in the context of emerging issues. Multi-stakeholder deliberation in the policy design process, or directed in policy content, allows for stakeholders with diverse information and expertise relating to a particular policy domain to exchange insights about current and evolving issues and the effectiveness of policies in the context of such. Self-organization, again in either the process of policy designing or as encouraged in the content of policy design, Swanson et al. argue engenders the development of social capital. They further argue that this, in turn, improves stakeholders' ability to respond to unexpected events through novel policy approaches (Swanson et al., 2010, p. 932). Decentralization in policy process and content allows for those most proximate to policy issues to advise on their nuances and changing qualities. Finally, Swanson et al. suggest the possibility of implementing multiple policies simultaneously that may be more or less effective in responding to different policy scenarios.

A key summary point to this section is that thinking about policy design in adaptive terms layers traditional ways of thinking about policy effectiveness with new ones. Namely, from this perspective, effective policies are not necessarily those that yield desired outputs at one point in time, but rather are those that continue to be effective in the presence of dynamic contextual conditions. This notion of efficacy it tied to the concept of robustness, which has been of central import in scholarship on adaptive governance. In this scholarship, robustness refers to the ability to retain functionality in the presence of shocks, where shocks represent minor to major changes in social, physical, technological, and/or other conditions (Levin and Lubchenco, 2008; Howlett, 2019). The analogue in the policy design context is thus the sustained efficacy of policies even as the governing contexts in which they are applied change in various ways to varying extents.

Scholars have integrated the concept of robustness into their discussion of a new orientation in the study of policy design. As noted earlier in this Element, this new design orientation emphasizes the use and designs of policy bundles or mixes over single policies in the governance of issues and the need to account for uncertainty and complexity miring enduring and emerging governance challenges through policy design (Capano and Woo, 2018; Howlett, 2019). In positing a definition and the importance of policy robustness, Capano and Woo (2018) note the following with reference to recent financial and energy crises:

> To manage such uncertainty, policymaking needs to be capable of responding to unexpected events and their impacts, through the activation of different modes/mechanisms (i.e., learning, adaptation, improvisation) to maintain their commitment and effectiveness in pursuing the expected policy goals. This capacity of policymaking to respond to, and retain functionality amid, uncertainty can be defined as "robustness." ... Robustness applies to both

design process and design outputs, imbuing both with the capability to react to shock and uncertainty by maintaining functionality. In other words, robustness can be a powerful driver of policy effectiveness and functionality over time. ... This role of robustness is particularly important in light of the increasingly complex and unstable policy environment that policymakers are faced with.

In characterizing factors that contribute to robust policy designs, Capano and Woo note many of the same factors referenced by DeCaro et al. (2017), including stakeholder engagement and other mechanisms of decentralized decision-making.

Howlett (2019) also discusses policy robustness, defining it in terms of enduring functionality in the context of shifting conditions, within the context of policy mixes specifically. Policy robustness is itself conceived of at the "mix" or "bundle" level. From Howlett's perspective, policy mixes are considered robust when the elements of the policies of which they are comprised are complementary or reinforcing. An additional dimension accounted for by Howlett in his conceptualization of policy robustness is temporality. The key point emphasized by Howlett regarding temporality, is that policies, even when existing within a mix, often have unique trajectories. Various factors influence when and how policies change, and changes to different policies within mixes are often not coordinated. The implication of having policies within mixes that exhibit different trajectories in terms of how they change over time, is that the extent of robustness of policies may fluctuate over time.

3.2.2 Operationalizing Adaptability through Policy Design

Leveraging the work referenced in the previous section, the policy analyst is equipped with some theoretical and conceptual guidance for operationalizing policy adaptability through assessments of policy design. Indeed, analyzing policy designs with the intent of assessing adaptability is logical since it is through them that policymakers specify channels of information flow, establish protocols for collective decision-making, offer instructions for policy implementation, and structure opportunities and incentives for public participation (Schneider and Ingram, 1997; Ostrom, 2005). Even more specifically, through examinations of policy design, one can determine whether a policy contains features of an adaptive policy highlighted by scholars in the preceding section; for example, whether it relies on proportional rather than fixed standards, incorporates planned periods of comprehensive evaluation (e.g., legal sunsets), uses institutionalized authority for local autonomy to promote responsiveness to local conditions, creates opportunities for public participation, establishes external and internal monitoring and enforcement mechanisms, includes policy triggers that adjust performance standards based on policy or contextual feedback, and accommodates decentralization in decision-making to the lowest and most effective jurisdictional level (Swanson et al., 2010; DeCaro et a., 2017).

Meso- and micro-level approaches for analyzing policy design can be informative in considering how to operationalize policy adaptability through policy design. One could, for example, use Ostrom's approach that organizes directives comprising public policies into their functional properties, such as whether they address collective decision-making and activity or how information is communicated among policy relevant actors. To remind, under Ostrom's approach, collective decision-making is indicated through aggregation rules. Channels of information flow are specified by information rules. A more precise understanding of the features of adaptive policy design could be achieved through the application of micro-level approaches. Leveraging the institutional grammar, for example, the analysts could also glean a richer and systematic understanding of not only whether policy designs accommodate diverse stakeholder participation, but also the specific conditions under which it is required, permitted, or forbidden to occur. As another example, leveraging this approach, the analyst could also precisely identify the specific conditions under which specified policy triggers are required, permitted, or forbidden to take effect. Such examples are simply intended to illustrate the analytical capacity that meso- and micro-level approaches covered previously offer in the operationalization of adaptability within the context of policy design.

4 Analyzing Policy Design Across Levels

Section 2 of this Element presents structural features of policy design. It highlights generalizable features of policies that associate with different analytical levels: the macro, meso, and micro levels. A summary of key points relating to analyzing policy design at different levels based on the discussion provided earlier is provided below. This is followed by an illustrative analysis of the design of policies governing the aquaculture industry in the state of Colorado, United States, which highlights the analytical leverage one derives from evaluating policy designs at different levels.

The aquaculture policy case was selected for the purpose of analytical illustration for multiple reasons. First, the primary objective of the two policies examined is to establish parameters for aquaculture-related behavior; that is, to compel behaviors of various kinds. This quality of the policies makes them more amenable to analyses based on the macro-, meso-, and particularly, micro-level approaches addressed in this Element. By way of contrast, the objective of some policies is simply to define or establish policy-relevant states, properties, entities, etc., within a particular domain, in other words, to "constitute" them. While one can certainly engage in macro-, meso-, or micro-level assessments of either more constitutive or regulatory (i.e., policies aimed at opportuning or constraining behavior) policies, one will likely find that approaches situating at different levels reviewed in this Element are better suited to the latter. This perception has been expressed by scholars employing the institutional grammar (Siddiki et al., 2019). A second reason the aquaculture case is appropriate for an analytical illustration is that both policies examined are sufficiently elaborate that one can observe within them various types of directives that can be categorized at the meso and micro level. Leveraging Ostrom's rule typology, for example, one will find in these policies directives that associate with multiple rule types. There are thus more analytical possibilities with these types of policies than with less well-developed policies that may contain fewer directives, and thus likely fewer directives of different kinds. A third reason for using the aquaculture case is simply the growing salience of aquaculture production at the state, national, and international scales. As noted by Ottinger et al. (2016), aquaculture is the fastest growing animal food production sector worldwide, being viewed as an effective strategy for dealing with depleting wild fish stocks, food insecurity, and rising seafood demand. In the United States, aquaculture policymaking is largely devolved to the state level. The assessment here provides insights into how one state has decided to regulate the increasingly prominent aquaculture sector; including insights on, for example, the types of actors impacted by policy and the scope of activities regulated therewith.

Macro-level characterizations of policy design are the broadest in scope, and typically involve classifying whole policies in terms of type. Leading policy typologies supporting macro-level assessments of policy design typically rely on policy function, allocation of resources, or political antecedents or consequences, as a basis for classification. Macro-level assessments of policy design can be particularly useful for inter-policy comparisons; that is, for thinking about how different policies are distinct in their intent, as well as how they relate to each other. Meso-level assessments focus on elements of design that are common across policies observed in different domains. Meso-level assessments of policy design move attention from policies as a whole, as is given when applying a macro-level lens to the study of policy design, to the specific directives that comprise policies and the content conveyed through them. Leading approaches for meso-level studies of policy design offer a basis for characterizing these directives, independently or in configurations, along some bases. The two meso-level analysis approaches reviewed in this element, by Ostrom (2005) and Schneider and Ingram (1997), use the functional properties of policy directives as a basis for organizing them. Meso-level approaches offer distinct analytical utility relative to macro-level approaches. Whereas macro-level approaches focus primarily on inter-policy classification, meso-level approaches also enable intra-policy assessments; that is, assessments of how the various directives that comprise policies fit together, or cohere, in accordance with broader policy goals or objectives. Thus, beyond yielding descriptive insights about the structure of policy designs, meso-level approaches also support evaluations of the quality of policy designs.

Micro-level assessments of policy design offer more granular depictions of policy design than meso-level, and certainly macro-level approaches. Like meso-level approaches, micro-level approaches focus on directives constituting policies. However, unlike meso-level approaches that classify entire directives in accordance with some criteria, micro-level approaches provide a basis for classifying content within directives. They draw attention to elements common to directives within and across policies, and it is along these elements that directive content is categorized. These elements are often represented as different syntactic elements. The micro-level approach reviewed in this Element, for example, provides guidance for classifying the content of directives according to the action indicated in the statement; the actor associated with this action;, a prescriptive operator that indicates whether the actor is required, forbidden or allowed to perform the action; the temporal, spatial, and/or procedural conditions associated with the action; and payoffs associated with the action. Like meso-level approaches, micro-level approaches for analyzing policy design enable inter- and intra-policy evaluations.

Having provided a summary of key points relating to macro, meso, and micro assessments of policy design, the remainder of the section will offer an illustrative policy design analysis that showcases the types of insights that derive from assessments oriented at different levels. Two policies are analyzed for this illustration. Both govern the aquaculture industry in the state of Colorado, USA: one being the primary legislation that governs the aquaculture industry – the "Colorado Aquaculture Act" – and the other being the corresponding regulation developed by the Colorado Department of Agriculture that provides guidance on the implementation and enforcement of the Colorado Aquaculture Act – the "Rules Pertaining to Administration and Enforcement of the Colorado Aquaculture Act." The primary objectives of the Colorado Aquaculture Act are to establish aquaculture as a regulated industry by the state, identify the primary roles and responsibilities of the Commissioner of Agriculture in relation to the regulation of the aquaculture industry, establish criteria of eligibility for becoming a permitted aquaculture producer, and outline general sanctions for violations of legal standards. The Colorado Aquaculture Act also establishes and outlines the responsibilities of the Colorado Aquaculture Board, an entity made up of government officials and members of the aquaculture industry that provides guidance to the Commissioner of Agriculture on the regulation of the aquaculture industry and aquaculture markets. The Rules Pertaining to the Administration and Enforcement of the Colorado Aquaculture Act contains specific instructions for obtaining an aquaculture permit, the inspection of aquaculture facilities to ensure their compliance with regulatory standards, record keeping by aquaculture facilities regarding the acquisition, trade, sale, and disposition of aquatic organisms, and penalties for regulatory noncompliance.

The following macro-, meso-, and micro-level approaches for analyzing policy design are used in the evaluation of the design of the two aquaculture policies described below. The macro-level assessment is based on Lowi's policy typology, which classifies policies as regulatory, redistributive, or redistributive. The meso-level assessment is based on Ostrom's rule typology, according to which behavioral (e.g., policy) directives that constitute policies are characterized as being of seven types based on their functional properties: scope rules (identify required, desired or prohibited outcomes), choice rules (specify specific actions), information rules (govern communication and information flows), aggregation rules (address collective decision-making and activity), payoff rules (assign rewards or sanctions for specific actions), position rules (identify roles to be filled by individuals), and boundary rules (identify prerequisites for occupying positions). The micro-level assessment is based on Crawford and Ostrom's institutional grammar, which organizes the content of directives along the following syntactic elements, each of which conveys different semantic meaning relevant to the focus of the directive: Attribute (conveys to whom the directive applies and who performs the action indicated in the directive), Aim (action indicated in the directive), Object (the animate or inanimate receiver of the action in the statement), Deontic (prescriptive operator that indicates whether the action indicated in the directive is required, permitted or forbidden), Condition (the temporal, spatial or procedural condition(s) associated with the action), and Or else (payoff associated with performing, or not performing, the action indicated in the directive).

For the macro-level analysis of the Colorado Aquaculture Act and accompanying rules based on Lowi's typology, the policies, in their entirety, were considered for their core function. For the meso-level analysis, each of the two policies was parsed into individual behavioral directives and then these directives were classified according to Ostrom's rule typology. Policy documents were then summarized by rule type. For the purposes of the analysis, a directive was defined as a clause within the policy that, at least, indicates an action, an actor associated with the action, and a condition associated with the action. It could additionally contain a prescriptive operator and payoff associated with the action. In most cases, these clauses were coterminous with sentences, but not always. For the micro-level analysis, each directive was further dissected and organized in accordance with Crawford and Ostrom's institutional grammar syntax. Table 3 provides an illustration of how a portion of text from the Rules of Administration and Enforcement of the Colorado Aquaculture Act was dissected into individual directives, and then further parsed according to the institutional grammar syntax to support meso- and micro-level policy design analyses.

In summarizing the micro-coded data, attention was given to identifying and summarizing modal Attributes (i.e., Attributes appearing most frequently across policy directives), modal Objects (i.e., Objects appearing most frequently across policy directives), and statements containing "must," "must not," "may," and "may not" Deontics. Summarizing modal Attributes offers insights about the key targets of a policy. Summarizing modal Objects offers insights about the focal topics of a policy. Summarizing statements by the presence of certain types of Deontics conveys information about the level of behavioral discretion afforded to different policy targets through a particular policy. As noted previously in this Element, a core function of public policies is to compel the behavior of policy targets in accordance with policy goals, making behavioral discretion a critical dimension of policy design to analyze.

Figure 1 provides a descriptive summary of the macro-, meso-, and micro-level classification of the two policies. Reviewing the overarching objectives and functions of both the Colorado aquaculture legislation and corresponding regulation in relation to Lowi's macro-level policy typology, it is clear that both policies are regulatory in type. They are both designed primarily to manage the behavior of actors within the aquaculture industry context (including, for example, government actors and aquaculture producers) so as to prevent negative externalities of aquaculture production and sale. Results from the meso- and micro-level analyses of the policies' designs gives further insights about the functions of the aquaculture policies. An intra-policy assessment yields the following information. The Colorado Aquaculture Act (legislation) is composed of a total of fifty-nine directives. Results from the modal Attribute analysis show that the majority of directives govern the behavior and activities of the Commissioner of Agriculture, the Colorado Aquaculture Board, and the General Assembly. Directives pertaining to the General Assembly tend to refer to this entity's role in establishing the industry and conveying the rights and responsibilities of different actors in relation to the legislation. Results from the modal Object analysis show that primary topics addressed in directives include governing rules, permit suspensions and revocations, and powers of the

Table 3 Dissecting Policy Content

Regulatory Clause	Dissecting Regulatory Clause into Individual Directives	Dissecting Individual Directives According to Institutional Grammar Syntax
Except as prohibited by law, an [aquaculture] permittee may operate a fish production facility for the purposes of propagating, selling, trading, or transporting live fish or viable gametes. Several satellite stations of a fish production facility may operate under one aquaculture facility permit provided all such satellite stations are listed on such permit. All production facilities that sell or stock live fish shall obtain an annual fish health inspection performed by a qualified fish pathologist in accordance with Division [of Wildlife] regulations and policies.	[1] Except as prohibited by law, an [aquaculture] permittee may operate a fish production facility for the purposes of propagating, selling, trading, or transporting live fish or viable gametes. [2] Several satellite stations of a fish production facility may operate under one aquaculture facility permit provided all such satellite stations are listed on such permit.	[1] Attribute: Aquaculture permittee Deontic: may Aim: operate Object: a fish production facility Condition: for the purposes of propagating, selling, trading, or transporting live fish of viable gametes Or Else: N/A [2] Attribute: Aquaculture permittee (implied from preceding directive) Deontic: may Aim: operate Object: several satellite stations of a fish production facility Condition: under on aquaculture facility permit provided all such satellite stations are listed on such permit Or Else: N/A

[3]
All production facilities that sell or stock live fish shall obtain an annual fish health inspection performed by a qualified fish pathologist in accordance with Division [of Wildlife] regulations and policies.

[3]
Attribute: All production facilities that sell or stock live fish
Deontic: shall
Aim: obtain
Object: an annual fish health inspection performed by a qualified fish health pathologist in accordance with Division regulations and policies
Condition: annually
Or Else: N/A

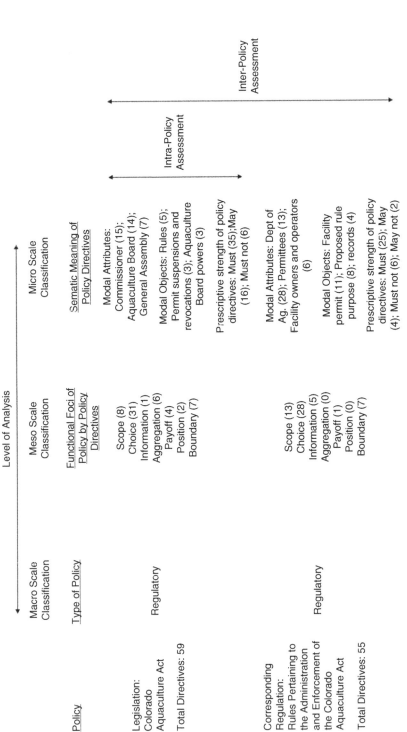

Figure 1 Analyzing Policy Design at the Macro, Meso, and Micro Scales: Illustration using Colorado Aquaculture Legislation and Corresponding Regulation

aquaculture board. Most of the directives in the legislation are choice rules indicating specific activities pertaining to these topics and assigned to modal Attributes. After choice rules, scope rules and boundary rules are the directives that appear with the greatest frequency. This finding accords with some of the core foci of the legislation – to establish the aquaculture industry as one regulated under the state of Colorado, and to establish criteria of eligibility for becoming a permitted aquaculture producer. Reviewing Deontics occurring frequently across policy directives reveals that little behavioral discretion is afforded to policy targets; over two-thirds of directives are requiring or forbidding activities through the use of "must" and "must not" Deontics, respectively.

The intra-policy assessment of the Rules Pertaining to the Administration and Enforcement of the Colorado Aquaculture Act (regulation corresponding to the Colorado Aquaculture Act) reveals the following information. The regulation is comprised of fifty-five directives. Results from the modal Attribute analysis show that the vast majority of directives govern the behavior and activities of the Department of Agriculture, aquaculture permittees, and facility owners and operators. Results from the modal Object analysis show that the primary topics addressed in the directives are facility permits, specification of the core purposes of the regulation, and records of aquatic organism sale, transport, and trade. The meso-level analysis, revealing the types of directives embodied in the regulation shows that most are choice rules that indicate specific activities relating to these different topics, and assigned to modal Attributes. After Choice rules, the next most frequently occurring types of directives (in order of highest to lowest frequency) are scope rules, boundary rules, and information rules. Consistent with the findings from the modal Object analysis, the scope rules present within the regulation largely focus on conveying the establishment of regulatory standards and foci. Consistent with the overall objective of the regulations, the boundary rules in the regulation identify who is/is not required to obtain an aquaculture permit. Finally, the information rules in the regulation address procedures for notifying aquaculture permit applicants of their approval/denial, communication of facility records of aquatic organisms, and transmission of invoices for the sale, trade, or disposition of aquatic organisms.

The inter-policy assessment of the aquaculture legislation and corresponding regulation also reveals interesting insights. The different policy targets and activities across two policy documents are logical given the varying foci of the policies. Differences in policy targets owing to different foci of the policies, as reflected in the Attribute analysis, are reflected in the rule types most common across the policy documents. For example, one of the core objectives of the Aquaculture Act is to establish the advisory rulemaking body, the Colorado Aquaculture Board, and its role in overseeing the Commissioner's decisions regarding permit suspensions and revocations. It is thus unsurprising that the Board is a modal Attribute in the regulation. The role of the Board, as connected to the focus of the Legislation, positions it as an entity that operates jointly with other actors and thus observed in the Legislation are aggregation rules, all of which mention activities performed jointly by members of the Aquaculture Board, or in conjunction with it. The Regulation, in contrast, contains no aggregation rules. Another contrast in the frequency of different types of rules across the policies revealed through the meso-level analysis, and that relates to the variable foci of the policies, is the greater number of payoff rules in the legislation relative to the regulation. One of the key objectives of the legislation is to outline general sanctions for violations of policy standards and thus one would expect to see payoff rules in this policy.

The policy design analysis offered in this section is primarily intended to be illustrative; to showcase how policies can be analyzed at different levels and the types of insights that derive from micro-, meso-, and macro-level policy assessments. This illustrative analysis also draws attention to types of insights that yield from inter- and intra-policy evaluations building on micro, meso, and macro assessments. Ultimately, how analysts approach their policy design evaluation – for example, on which particular data they focus their attention and how they interpret these data – will be guided by their specific research questions.

5 Future Directions for Policy Design Research

Presented in this section is guidance for future research on policy design leveraging ideas that have been presented throughout this Element. The recommendations are based in particular on the discussion of structural features and related assessments of policy design, policy compatibility, and policy adaptability.

5.1 Future Research Relating to the Structural Features of Policy Design

The discussion on policy design structure presented in this Element centers on analytical levels; that is, identifying and describing different analytical levels at which one can approach assessments of policy design. Underpinning this discussion is the argument that analyses oriented at different analytical levels offer alternative perspectives on policy design and yield results that vary in their generalizability across policy contexts. For example, micro-level analyses of the language of policies are usually conducted in the context of small-n case studies and offer nuanced descriptions and explanations of public policies in particular contexts. However, these studies are challenged by generalizability concerns. Macro-level analyses of policy design, in which policies are characterized broadly in terms of their function or intent, can support large-*n* comparative studies that generalize across policy contexts, but lack important nuance. Additionally, analyses oriented at different levels are also variably suited for enabling inter- and intra-policy design assessments. Meso- and micro-level analyses are particularly well suited for intra-policy assessments, though they can also be leveraged in comparing the precise designs of two or more policies.

Positioning assessments of policy design around levels of analysis provides one way of organizing the foci and contributions of extant theories, typologies, and studies of policy design. It can also be used as a basis for generating recommendations for future research on policy design. Much opportunity exists to develop theoretical and methodological approaches that associate with each level of analysis, as well as to further intellectual inquiry about the theoretical and methodological benefits and limitations of engaging in studies that apply, in concert, approaches that situate at different levels. Provided below are recommendations for future research engaging macro-, meso-, and micro-level approaches, as well as that which is based on cross-level assessments.

Posited earlier in this Element is that leading macro-level approaches for evaluating policy design offer useful heuristics for organizing types of policy based on general characterizations of their function, political contexts, and the ways in which they allocate resources among relevant policy targets, the first and last of which are essentially captured in policy design. Also noted in relation to these approaches is that a lack of specificity about the conceptual and operational criteria according to which policies can be categorized challenges their validity and utility. With only generally defined conceptual bases along which policies can be organized, which associates with typological overlap, the analyst confronts ambiguity in classification of a policy to a single category. The lack of operational guidance linked to conceptual classification – for example, guidance on specific features policy design or political context that can signal belonging of a policy into one typological category versus another – contributes to this sense of ambiguity.

Future policy design research can help address the limitations noted in the preceding paragraph in two different, albeit complementary, ways. One way is to pursue conceptual and theory development around existing policy typologies, with the former being a critical building block for the latter. Conceptual development would focus on clarifying and more fully articulating the bases of classification relating to different typologies, such that conceptual overlap between policy types is either resolved or more fully understood. It may not be possible, or even desirable, or eliminate overlap. When categorizing entire policies into one bin or another, it is likely implausible to identify features that make them wholly distinct. However, if there were more clarity on dimensions of concepts used for the purpose of differentiating one type of policy from another, the analyst could then note which dimensions policies are overlapping and/or distinct. Theoretical development would beg clarification on the logic and or mechanisms that relate policy type to something else, for example, features of the political context. The other related way to develop macro-level approaches for analyzing policy design would be to develop "coding guidelines" that articulate practical strategies for differentiating between types of policies. This would require specifying some empirical anchor to which such strategies could be tied, of which policy design is an appropriate one. Using policy design as an anchor, scholars could identify general features of policy design that signal that a policy is of one kind or another. These features would be more general than those offered through meso- and micro-level approaches, while still being rooted in policy content.

Meso-level approaches for assessing policy design explicitly prompt the analyst's attention to the content of policies. Generally, instead of offering some bases for categorizing whole policies in accordance with some criteria like macro-level approaches, meso-level approaches offer a basis for organizing the individual directives that comprise policies. The organizational scheme offered through these approaches is intended to be generalizable; in other words, be applicable to policies that differ in function, domain (e.g., education, health, environment), and substantive qualities. An assumption underlying these approaches is that policies are generally constituted of varying numbers of certain types of directives that vary in substantively meaningful ways (i.e., in terms of the functional properties or types of information they convey). Another important, and related, assumption is that directives of different types operate configurally to transmit policy-relevant information to policy targets. Using Ostrom's (2005) meso-level rule typology, for example, a particular policy may include position rules that describe the available positions for different types of policy targets within a particular setting (e.g., slots open for government and nongovernment actors on an advisory board) and these position rules are interpretable in connection with boundary rules embedded in the same policy that identify eligibility criteria for occupying those positions. Understanding the configural nature of directives comprising policy documents is critical for engaging in, and appreciating, the value of intra-policy assessments. As noted earlier in this Element, it is important for evaluating the coherence of public policies (i.e., how different directives fit together).

A question for the policy design analyst in conducting meso-level analyses is how to interpret descriptive summaries of policies, by type of descriptive, or even descriptive portrayals of how different types of directives link together – in form or in substance. No doubt this type of descriptive information is meaningful and important, but as scholars of public policy, there is often further motivation to interpret this information in normative terms. In other words, to understand what patterns observed through descriptive summaries of directives by type or configurations means for governance more broadly. This latter point offers a basis for a recommendation for future policy design–related research focused on applying or developing meso-level approaches. The recommendation, building off recent research conducted by Hanlon et al. (Forthcoming), is to develop concepts and theory for grounding and interpreting patterns among policy directives. Conceptual development, as was done by Hanlon et al., would involve operationalizing important governance concepts based on the presence or absence of certain types of directives or configurations of directives. Hanlon et al., for example, use configurations of directives in the operationalization of the concept of "credible commitment" in their examination of water governance policies. In other words, they argue and empirically demonstrate that credible commitment is indicated by the presence of a certain combination of directives of different types. Their work leverages Ostrom's rule typology. Theoretical development relating to the recommendation offered here would involve clarifying, and empirically testing, the logic and mechanisms that link patterns in types and configurations of directives to specific antecedents or outcomes.

Micro-level approaches for evaluating policy design are effective for gaining comprehensive understanding of the content of each directive included within a policy, as they require the analyst to dissect each part of the directive and organize it in accordance with a generalizable syntax. The value of micro-level approaches is the precision with which they capture features of policy design. Analysts applying micro-level approaches have at their disposal information about the number of directives constituting a policy, as well as about the linguistic properties of each directive, the latter of which convey policy-relevant semantic meaning. In existing scholarship applying the micro-level analytical approach featured in this Element – the Institutional Grammar – these "micro" data are clearly recognized as valuable. At the same time, the collection, analysis, and interpretation of these micro data are noted as challenging the broader appeal and use of micro-level approaches. Analysts note the significant time investment associated with micro-level characterizations of policy directives, which in nearly all applications to date has been a manual exercise. The possibility of automating this process is possible, and is an effort currently being pursued by various teams of scholars working with the Institutional Grammar. The analytical and interpretation challenges relating to micro-level approaches are akin to those observed with meso-level approaches; basically, that the analyst is left with large amounts of descriptive data that can only be meaningfully interpreted through a clearly articulated conceptual and/or theoretical lens. In the case of the Institutional Grammar specifically, for example, the analyst has, from the application thereof, large amounts of essentially parts-of-speech data, which offer little utility when interpreted independently, but can offer useful substantive insights when aggregated and configured. Key questions for the analyst are thus how to aggregate and configure these data to unveil these insights.

In light of what is noted previously, one recommendation for future policy design research based on micro-level approaches is to develop conceptual and theoretical approaches that can guide the interpretation of micro-policy data. The call here resembles that made in relation to meso-level approaches. Concept or theory development in the context of both cases should start with any existing conceptual or theoretical underpinnings of the different approaches. Schneider and Ingram's and Ostrom's meso-level approaches are rooted in theories of democratic governance and collective action respectively, which analysts availing the recommendation posed here should consider as a starting place in their efforts. Similarly, the Institutional Grammar is fundamentally grounded in assumptions about how individuals respond to different forms of prescriptive operators (e.g., must, may, must not) and material (and nonmaterial) incentives. Thus, those interested in theoretical development around the Institutional Grammar should at least consider how these theories inform the semantic logic, and associated syntax, articulated therein.

A final recommendation for future policy design–related research is to engage in cross-level analyses of policy design. Cross-level analyses offer several benefits. First, the simultaneous application of approaches that correspond to different analytical levels allows the analyst to overcome general limitations of individually applying micro, meso, or macro approaches. Second, cross-level assessments enable the analyst to think through how insights derived at one level of analysis translate up or down to other levels (Jilke et al., Forthcoming). This can be useful for the purpose of validation (i.e., assessing whether findings derived from analyses situated at different levels are coherent). Additionally, where this cross-level analysis is theoretically guided, it can foster theory building by clarifying the explanatory scope of concepts, propositions, and findings. In other words, it forces the analyst to consider at what level their theory operates and whether the theory accommodates drawing implications about how findings deriving from its application can be translated up or down across levels.

5.2 Future Research Relating to Policy Compatibility

Another major focus of this Element connecting policy design and policy efficacy is policy compatibility. The discussion in this Element focuses on two types of policy compatibility: inter-policy compatibility and intra-policy compatibility. Inter-policy compatibility refers to the extent of alignment on policy design elements (e.g., goals, instruments, incentives, syntactic elements) among policies that govern common and different subjects, targets, and policy issues. Intra-policy compatibility relates to the soundness of the causal logic embedded within policy designs that links policy goals, targets, and instruments and the behavioral tendencies of policy targets. The discussion of inter-policy compatibility presented in the Element builds from recent policy design and policy process scholarship that recognizes that policy issues are typically managed through suites of related policies. This observation naturally prompts inquiry on compatibility among the designs of policies applied simultaneously to common policy targets, subjects, and/or issues; that is, studies that investigate interactions among policy designs and the implications thereof. The focus on intra-policy compatibility is motivated by emphasis placed on this in prominent scholarship on design, for example, work by Schneider and Ingram (1997).

Existing scholarship has provided the rationale for focusing on inter- and intra-policy compatibility. In the case of intra-policy compatibility, scholars have even begun to present a conceptual and theoretical logic relating thereto. However, additional efforts directed at conceptual, theoretical, and also operational development relating to both types of compatibility are needed. While it is increasingly recognized that policymakers govern single domains through "bundles of policies" with varying degrees of attention to whether elements of these policies are compatible or conflicting, and thus assessments of compatibility are worthwhile, theoretical guidance regarding what types of policy interactions are likely to be most impactful is lacking. Put another way, in terms used to discuss the structural features of policy design in this Element, it is not clear on which policy design elements it is more or less important to have compatibility across policies, and what design and contextual factors might punctuate or dampen the effects of varying degrees of policy compatibility. The recommendation to pursue cross-level assessments of policy design is also relevant here. Engaging in cross-level assessments of inter-policy compatibility – for example, jointly applying a meso- and micro-level approach – would shed light on the relative value of assessing compatibility among meso-level and micro-level features of policy design. Theoretical development relating to the concept of intra-policy compatibility could focus on developing an elaborated articulation of how and why coherence among specific features of policy design is normatively more advantageous for governance. Further, theory development could focus on clarifying the mechanisms that link alignment between a policy's embedded causal logic and behavioral tendencies of policy targets to outcomes of interest.

5.3 Future Research Relating to Policy Adaptability

This Element highlights the importance of policy adaptability in relation to policy efficacy, essentially positing that policies that are designed to be adaptable, or to facilitate adaptability in governance in response to new information, are likely to be more effective. Further argued is that policy adaptability is generally important given that the contexts in which they are applied are inherently dynamic, but that this quality of policies is increasingly important given the complexity and uncertainty that characterizes some of the most pressing challenges we face in modern governance. The section on policy adaptability in this Element presents various ways that policies can be designed to encourage adaptation or receptivity to new information, the latter of which enables the former.

Future research on policy adaptability approached through the lens of policy design should build on recent scholarship that highlights various characteristics of policy that facilitate adaptability to articulate how these characteristics can be operationalized and systematically assessed through policy design. Scholars can leverage the existing macro-, meso-, and micro-level approaches reviewed in this Element, or others, in this pursuit. Leveraging existing approaches would require thinking and offering operational guidance about how features and information about policies identified through their application can be used to identify and understand characteristics of policy that encourage adaptability. For example, DeCaro et al. (2017) identifies the following characteristics of policies that enable adaptive governance: reflexivity, formal delegation of authority, formal delegation of responsibility, and tangible support. The task for scholars suggested here is that one think, for example, about whether and how an assessment of policy directives in terms of their functional properties (meso-level analysis) or the semantically parsed content of individual directives (micro-level analysis) can be used to detect the presence of these policy characteristics. If policy design scholars develop ways to assess policy adaptability in operational terms, they will then be equipped to perform systematic empirical evaluations of the implications of adaptive governance mechanisms.

5.4 Concluding Remarks

In a 2014 article in *Policy Sciences*, Michael Howlett made the following claim:

> The real challenge for a new generation of design studies is to develop greater conceptual clarity and the methodological sophistication needed in order to sift through the complexity of new policy regimes, policy mixes, alternative instruments for governance, and changing governance networks and link these to a deeper theory of design.

In essence, this Element responds to Howlett's call. It outlines a multi-level analytical framework for organizing approaches for studying policy based on unit of analysis, which, in turn, fosters methodological clarity and appreciation of the analytical leverage of studies situated at different levels. Further, it offers an illustrative application of this multi-level framework. Even more broadly, the discussion offered in this Element, as well as the recommendations for future research offered in this section, reflect the importance of policy design in the broader study of governance. Further, they emphasize the need to have rigorous methods to engage in the study of policy design that are informed by sound conceptual and theoretical logic. With greater understanding of policy design, scholars will be better equipped to understand the implications thereof to then advance scholarship and advise practice. The discussion and recommendations contained herein also reflect an evolving trend in policy design scholarship, which is to structure studies to better reflect the complexity of policy contexts. This complexity owes in part to the increased use of policy bundles to govern in any domain, the inherent dynamism of social, physical, informational, and other contexts in which policies are applied, and uncertain conditions associated with the issues on which policymakers are being compelled to govern in our modern era. Effective governance in light of this complexity now and in the future hinges on effective policy design.

References

Anderson, C. W. (1977). *Statecraft: An Introduction to Political Choice and Judgement*. New York, NY: Wiley.

Basurto, X., Kingsley, G., McQueen, K., Smith, M., & Weible, C. M. (2010). A Systematic Approach to Institutional Analysis: Applying Crawford and Ostrom's Grammar. *Political Research Quarterly 63* (3), 523–537.

Beratan, K. K. (2007). A Cognition-Based View of Decision Processes in Complex Social-Ecological Systems. *Ecology and Society 12* (1), 27.

Birkland, T. A. (2011). *An Introduction to the Policy Process: Theories, Concepts, and Models of Public Policy Decision Making*, 3rd Edition. Armonk, NY: M.E. Sharpe.

Busetti, S., & Dente, B. (2016). Designing Multi-Actor Implementation: A Mechanism-Based Approach. *Public Policy and Administration 33* (1): 46–65.

Camerer, C., Issacharoff, S., Loewenstein, G., O'Donoghue, T., & Rabin, M. (2003). Regulation for Conservatives: Behavioral Economics and the Case for "Asymmetric Paternalism. *University of Pennsylvania Law Review 151* (3), 1211–1254.

Capano, G., & Woo, J.J. (2018). Designing Policy Robustness: Outputs and Processes. *Policy and Society 37* (4), 422–440.

Carter, David P., Christopher M. Weible, Saba N. Siddiki, and Xavier Basurto. 2016. "integrating Core Concepts from the Institutional Analysis and Development Framework for the Systematic Analysis of Policy Designs: An Illustration from the U.S. National Organic Program Regulation." *Regulation & Governance 28* (1): 159–185.

Chetty, R. (2015). Behavioral Economics and Public Policy: A Pragmatic Perspective. *American Economic Review 105* (5), 1–33.

Crawford, S. E., & Ostrom, E. (1995). A Grammar of Institutions. *The American Political Science Review 89* (3), 582–600.

Cushman, R. (1941). *The Independent Regulatory Commission*. London, UK: Oxford University Press.

DeCaro, D. (2018). Humanistic Rational Choice and Compliance Motivation in Complex Societal Dilemmas. In *Contextualizing Compliance in the Public Sector: Individual Motivations, Social Processes, and Institutional Design*, Saba Siddiki, Salvador Espinosa, and Tanya Heikkila, eds. New York, NY: Routledge, 126–147.

DeCaro, D., Chaffin, B. C., Schlager, E., Garmestani, A. S., & Ruhl, J. B. (2017). Legal and Institutional Foundations of Adaptive Environmental Governance. *Ecology & Society 22* (1), 1–32.

Doern, G. B., & Phidd, R. (1983). Canadian Public Policy: Ideas, Structure, and Process. Toronto, ON: Methuen.

Doremus, H. (2003). A Policy Portfolio Approach to Biodiversity Protection on Private Lands. *Environmental Science & Policy 6* (3), 217–232.

Edelman, M. (1985). *The Symbolic Uses of Politics*. Champaign, IL: University of Illinois.

Elmore, Richard F. (1987). Instruments and Strategy in Public Policy. *Policy Studies Review 7* (1), 174–186.

Gibson, Clark C., Elinor Ostrom, and T.K. Ahn. 2000. "The Concept of Scale and the Human Dimensions of Change: A Survey." *Ecological Economics 32*: 217–239.

Gunningham, N., Grabosky, P., & Sinclair, D. (1998). Smart Regulation. *Regulatory Theory*: 133.

Gunningham, Neil and Darren Sinclair. 1999. "Regulatory Pluralism: Designing Policy Mixes for Environmental Protection." *Law & Policy 21* (1): 49-76.

Hanlon, J., Olivier, T., & Schlager, E. (Forthcoming). Suspicious Collaborators: How Government in Polycentric Systems Monitor Behavior and Enforce Public Good Provision Against One Another. *International Journal of the Commons*.

Hood, C. (1986). *The Tools of Government*. London, UK: Chatham House Publishers.

Hood, C. (2007). Intellectual Obsolescence and Intellectual Makeovers: Reflections on the Tools of Government after Two Decades. *Public Administration Review* 20 (1), 127–144.

Howlett, M. (2018). Matching Policy Tools and Their Targets: Beyond Nudges and Utility Maximization in Policy Design. *Policy & Politics 46* (1), 101–124.

Howlett, N. (2019). Procedural Policy Tools and the Temporal Dimensions of Policy Design. *International Review of Public Policy 1* (1), Online.

Howlett, M. & Mukherjee, I. (2017). Policy Design: From Tools to Patches. *Canadian Public Administration 60* (1), 140–144.

Howlett, M. & Rayner, J. (2007). Design Principles for Policy Mixes: Cohesion and Coherence in "New Governance Arrangements." *Policy and Society 26* (4), 1–18.

Howlett, M., Mukherjee, I. & Woo, J. J. (2015). From Tools to Toolkits in Policy Design Studies: The New Design Orientation towards Policy Formulation Research. *Policy & Politics 43* (2), 291–311.

Howlett, Michael. 2014. "From the 'Old' to the 'New' Policy Design: Design Thinking Beyond Markets and Collaborative Governance." *Policy Sciences 47*: 187–207.

Howlett, Michael and Ishani Mukherjee. 2014. "Policy Design: From Tools to Patches." *Canadian Public Administration 60* (1); 140–144.

Hutchins, E. (1995). *Cognition in the Wild*. Cambridge, MA: MIT Press.

Jenkins-Smith, H. C., Nohrstedt, D., Weible, C. M., & Ingold, K. (2018). The Advocacy Coalition Framework: An Overview of the Research Program. In *Theories of the Policy Process*, 4th Edition, C. M. Weible and P. A. Sabatier, eds. Boulder, CO: Westview Press, 135–172.

Jilke, S., Olsen, A. L., Resh, W., & Siddiki, S. (Forthcoming). Microbrook, Mesobrook, and Macrobrook. *Perspectives on Public Management and Governance.*

Jones, B. D. (2001). *Politics and the Architecture of Choice: Bounded Rationality and Governance*. Chicago, IL: University of Chicago Press.

Kassekert, A., & Feiock, R. C. (2009). Policy Tool Selection: Predicting the Bundling of Economic Development Policy Instruments Using Multivariate Probit Analysis. Presented at the American Political Science Association Annual Meeting. Toronto, Canada.

Kirschen, E. S. (1964). *Economic Policy in Our Time*s. Chicago, IL: University of Chicago Press.

Kiser, Larry L. and Elinor Ostrom. 1982. "The Three Worlds of Action: A Metatheoretical Synthesis of Institutional Approaches." In Elinor Ostrom, Ed., *Strategies of Political Inquiry*. Beverly Hills, CA: Sage Publications, pp. 179–222.

Laswell, H. (1936). *Politics: Who Gets What, When, and How*. Gloucester, MA: Peter Smith Publisher.

Levin, S. A., & Lubchenco, J. (2008). Resilience, Robustness, and Marine Ecosystem-Based Management. *Bioscience 58* (1), 27–32.

Linder, S. H., & Peters, B. G. (1989). Instruments of Government: Perceptions and Contexts. *Journal of Public Policy 9* (1), 35–58.

Loewenstein, G., & Chater, N. (2017). Putting Nudges in Perspective. *Behavioural Public Policy 1* (1), 26–53.

Lowi, T. J. (1964). American Business, Public Policy, Case Studies, and Political Theory. *World Politics 16* (4), 677–715.

Madrian, B. (2014). Applying Insights from Behavioral Economics to Policy Design. *Annual Review of Economics 6*, 663–688.

March, J. G., & Olsen, J. O. (1995). *Democratic Governance*. New York, NY: Free Press.

May, P. J., Sapotichne, J., & Workman, S. (2006). Policy Coherence and Policy Domains. *Policy Studies Journal 34* (3), 381–403.

Mondou, M., & Montpetit, E. (2010). Policy Styles and Degenerative Politics: Poverty Policy Designs in Newfoundland and Quebec. *Policy Studies Journal 38* (4), 703–722.

Mosher, Frederick C. 1980. "The Changing Responsibilities and Tactics of the Federal Government." *Public Administration Review 40* (6): 541–548.

Munro, G., & Ditto, P. H. (1997). Biased Assimilation, Attitude Polarization, and Affect in Reactions to Stereotype-Relevant Scientific Information. *Personality and Social Psychology Bulletin 23* (6), 636–653.

Ostrom, E. (2005). *Understanding Institutional Diversity.* Princeton, NJ: Princeton University Press.

Ostrom, V. (1962). The Water Economy and Its Organization. *Natural Resources Journal 2* (1), 55–73.

Pierson, P. (1993). When Effect Becomes Cause: Policy Feedback and Political Change. *World Politics 45* (4), 595–628.

Ryan, R. M., & Deci, E. L. (2000). Self-Determination Theory and the Facilitation of Intrinsic Motivation, Social Development, and Well-Being. *American Psychologist 55* (1), 68–78.

Sabatier, P., & Mazmanian, D. (1980). The Implementation of Public Policy: A Framework of Analysis. *Policy Studies Journal.*

Salamon, L. M. (1989). *Beyond Privatization: The Tools of Government Action.* Washington, DC: The Urban Institute Press.

Salamon, L. M. (2002). *The Tools of Government: A Guide to the New Governance.* Oxford, UK: Oxford University Press.

Schlager, E., & Cox, M. (2018). The IAD Framework and the SES Framework: An Introduction and Assessment of the Ostrom Workshop Frameworks. In *Theories of the Policy Process*, 4th Edition. C. M. Weible and P. A. Sabatier, eds. Boulder, CO: Westview Press, 215–252.

Schneider, A., & Ingram, H. (1988). Systematically Pinching Ideas: A Comparative Approach to Policy Design. *Journal of Public Policy 8* (1), 61–80.

Schneider, A., & Ingram, H. (1990). Behavioral Assumptions of Policy Tools. *The Journal of Politics 52* (2), 510–529.

Schneider, A. L., & Ingram, H. (1997). *Policy Design for Democracy.* Lawrence, KS: University of Kansas Press.

Siddiki, S. (2014). Assessing Policy Design and Interpretation: An Institutions-Based Analysis in the Context of Aquaculture in Florida and Virginia, United States. *Regulation & Governance 31* (4), 281–303.

Siddiki, S. (2018). Policy Design and Conflict. In *Routledge Handbook of Policy Design.* M. Howlett and I. Mukherjee, eds. New York, NY: Routledge, 212–224.

Siddiki, S., Carley, S., Zirogiannis, N., Duncan, D., & Graham, J. (2018). Does Dynamic Federalism Yield Compatible Policies? A Study of the Designs of Federal and State Vehicle Policies. *Policy Design and Practice 1* (3), 215–232.

Siddiki, S., Frey, S., Rice, D., Schlager, E., & Schweik, C.M. (2019). *Research Coordination Network: Coordinating and Advancing Analytical Approaches for Policy Design*. United States National Science Foundation proposal.

Siddiki, S., Heikkila, T., Weible, C. M., Pacheco-Vega, R., Carter, D., Curley, C., DeSlatte, A., & Bennett, A. (2019). Institutional Analysis with the Institutional Grammar. *Policy Studies Journal.* Online first.

Siddiki, S., Weible, C. M., Basurto, X., & Calanni, J. (2011). Dissecting Policy Designs: An Application of the Institutional Grammar Tool. *Policy Studies Journal 39* (1), 79–103.

Siddiki, Saba, Tanya Heikkila, Christopher M. Weible, Raul Pacheco-Vega, David Carter, Cali Curley, Aaron DeSlatte, and Abby Bennett. 2019. "Institutional Analysis with the Institutional Grammar." *Policy Studies Journal.* Online first.

Siddiki, Saba, Xavier Basurto, and Christopher M. Weible. 2012. "Using the Institutional Grammar Tool to Understand Regulatory Compliance: The Case of Colorado Aquaculture." *Regulation & Governance 6*: 167–188.

Simon, H. A. (1979). Rational Decision Making in Business Organizations. *American Economic Review 69* (4), 493–513.

Simon, H.A. 1957. Models of Man, Social and Rational: Mathematical Essays on Rational Human Behavior in a Social Setting. New York, NY: Wiley.

Skocpol, T. (1992). *Protecting Soldiers and Mothers: The Political Origins of Social Policy in the United States*. Cambridge, MA: Cambridge University Press.

Smith, K. B. (2002). Typologies, Taxonomies, and the Benefits of Policy Classification. *Policy Studies Journal 30* (2), 379–395.

Steinberger, P. J. (1980). Typologies for Public Policy: Meaning Construction and the Policy Process. *Social Science Quarterly 61* (2), 185–197.

Swanson, D., Barg, S., Tyler, S., Venema, H., Tomar, S., Bhadwal, S., Nair, S., Roy, D., & Drexhage, J. (2010). Seven Tools for Creating Adaptive Policies. *Technological Forecasting & Social Change 77*, 924–939.

Thaler, R., & Sunstein, C. (2008). *Nudge: Improving Decisions about Health, Wealth, and Happiness*. New Haven, CT: Yale University Press.

Weible, C. M., & Carter, D. (2015). The Composition of Policy Change: Comparing Colorado's 1997 and 2006 Smoking Bans. *Policy Sciences 48*, 207–231.

Weimer, D. L., & Vining, A. R. (2011). *Policy Analysis: Concepts and Practice*, 5th Edition. New York, NY: Routledge Press.

Wilson, J. Q. (1974). *Political Organizations*. New York, NY: Basic Books.

Yi, H., & Feiock, R. C. (2012). Pool Tool Interactions and the Adoption of State Renewable Portfolio Standards. *Review of Policy Research 29* (2), 193–206.

Young, O. R. (2002). *The Institutional Dimensions of Environmental Change: Fit, Interplay, and Scale*. Cambridge, MA: MIT Press.

Cambridge Elements ☰

Public Policy

M. Ramesh

National University of Singapore (NUS)

M. Ramesh is UNESCO Chair on Social Policy Design at the Lee Kuan Yew School of Public Policy, NUS. His research focuses on governance and social policy in East and Southeast Asia, in addition to public policy institutions and processes. He has published extensively in reputed international journals. He is co-editor of Policy and Society and Policy Design and Practice.

Michael Howlett

Simon Fraser University, British Colombia

Michael Howlett is Burnaby Mountain Professor and Canada Research Chair (Tier 1) in the Department of Political Science, Simon Fraser University. He specializes in public policy analysis, and resource and environmental policy. He is currently editor-in-chief of *Policy Sciences* and co-editor of the *Journal of Comparative Policy Analysis; Policy and Society* and *Policy Design and Practice*.

Xun Wu

Hong Kong University of Science and Technology

Xun Wu is Professor and Head of the Division of Public Policy at the Hong Kong University of Science and Technology. He is a policy scientist whose research interests include policy innovations, water resource management and health policy reform. He has been involved extensively in consultancy and executive education, his work involving consultations for the World Bank and UNEP.

Judith Clifton

University of Cantabria

Judith Clifton is Professor of Economics at the University of Cantabria, Spain. She has published in leading policy journals and is editor-in-chief of the *Journal of Economic Policy Reform*. Most recently, her research enquires how emerging technologies can transform public administration, a forward-looking cutting-edge project which received €3.5 million funding from the Horizon2020 programme.

Eduardo Araral

National University of Singapore (NUS)

Eduardo Araral is widely published in various journals and books and has presented in forty conferences. He is currently Co-director of the Institute of Water Policy at the Lee Kuan Yew School of Public Policy, NUS, and is a member of the editorial board of *Journal of Public Administration Research and Theory* and the board of the Public Management Research Association.

About the series

Elements in Public Policy is a concise and authoritative collection of assessments of the state of the art and future research directions in public policy research, as well as substantive new research on key topics. Edited by leading scholars in the field, the series is an ideal medium for reflecting on and advancing the understanding of critical issues in the public sphere. Collectively, it provides a forum for broad and diverse coverage of all major topics in the field while integrating different disciplinary and methodological approaches.

Public Policy

Elements in the series

Printed in the United States
By Bookmasters